The
Self-Sufficient
HOME

This book was printed using responsible environmental practices by FSC-certified book manufacturers. The Forest Stewardship Council (FSC) encourages the responsible management of the world's forests. The Rainforest Alliance works to conserve biodiversity and ensure sustainable livelihoods by transforming land-use practices, business practices, and consumer behavior.

The
Self-Sufficient
HOME

Going Green and Saving Money

Christopher Nyerges

STACKPOLE
BOOKS

Published by
STACKPOLE BOOKS
5067 Ritter Road
Mechanicsburg, PA 17055
www.stackpolebooks.com

Printed in the United States of America

10 9 8 7 6 5 4 3 2 1

First edition

Cover design by Caroline M. Stover

Library of Congress Cataloging-in-Publication Data

Nyerges, Christopher.
    The self-sufficient home: going green and saving money / Christopher
    Nyerges.—1st ed.
        p. cm.
    Includes bibliographical references.
    ISBN-13: 978-0-8117-3558-2
    ISBN-10: 0-8117-3558-3
    1. Ecological houses. 2. Sustainable living. 3. Dwellings—Energy conservation.
    I. Title.

TH4860.N94 2009
640—dc22

2009000448

Acknowledgments

I thank everyone who assisted me in the preparation of this book—all the folks whose names appear throughout these pages. I especially thank Glenn Forbes, who spent so much time making sure I had the technical aspects correct in the solar electricity section. Everyone was so eager to share their stories and to be a part of this book. I sincerely thank you all!

I also give special thanks to my wife, Dolores, who lived so much of this with me, and to Revve Weisz, who taught me what it is to think.

Contents

OTHER BOOKS BY CHRISTOPHER NYERGES

Extreme Simplicity: Homesteading in the City
   (with Dolores Lynn Nyerges)

How to Survive Anywhere

Guide to Wild Foods and Useful Plants

Enter the Forest

Testing Your Outdoor Survival Skills

Urban Wilderness: A Guidebook to Resourceful City Living

Wild Greens and Salads: A Cookbook

Guide to Wild Foods

Foreword

Humans have walked this earth for over one million years. For practically all that time, we were hunter/gatherers—a hardy and self-reliant bunch that lived in relative harmony with our surroundings. Ten thousand years ago, for reasons that are still largely a mystery, a cataclysmic change in human behavior occurred. We started to farm and settle down. The leisurely two- or three-day "work week" of the hunter/gatherer was replaced by the endless year-round toil of the farmer. Around the Mediterranean, the sturdy frame of the hunter shrank by over twelve inches during the transition to farming, and health declined precariously. Cities soon arose, and the egalitarian and generalist ways of the hunter/gatherer were replaced by rigid hierarchies and specialization of labor. As society grew more complex, its citizens became more interdependent, and a sense of control over individual destinies was drastically diminished. Nature, to which we were once so intimately connected, became something to be feared, subdued, and exploited. It is ironic that the perceived security of civilization often turns out to be much less stable in the face of a natural disaster than the hunter/gatherer's way of life. The Bushmen, who once roamed across all of southern Africa, were long ago driven to one of the most inhospitable regions of the world—the Kalahari Desert—by more "culturally advanced" tribes. During a drought or other natural disaster, however, the Bushmen have a greater chance of survival than their farming Bantu neighbors. During the time that Native Americans were hunting bison, many regions of the American prairie were able to sustain a relatively large population density, yet the European settlers who displaced the natives had to abandon their farms within a few years.

Flash-forward to the early years of the twenty-first century. The Neolithic era has reached its zenith in the form of the nation-state. Across the globe, an exploding population has migrated to vast metropolitan areas. Communion with the natural world has become a rare event. Mankind finds itself surrounded by a man-made environment. A potted plant in the windowsill acts as surrogate for the forests and meadows of our past. All of this has taken place in the evolutionary blink of an eye. A mere ten thousand years of civilization is much too short of a time period to have any genetic influence on our hunter/gatherer brains. A zoo-born wolf will pace back and forth in its cage, longing for the forests and tundra it has never known. Similarly, many amongst us are pacing back and forth in our minds, longing for liberation from this Neolithic straitjacket, pining for Arcadia or Utopia, while an escalating frenzy of greed is laying waste to the world around us. Now, in these first years of the twenty-first century, things are coming to a head. Global warming, the despair of entire generations who have been displaced in their own countries, rampant financial malfeasance—we are all too familiar with the symptoms of our current crises. At the same time, there has never been a greater surge of innovation, with the promise of solutions to many of the problems facing us today. Alternative energy is rapidly approaching "grid parity," when it will be able to compete in the open market with coal and nuclear energy production. Two of the most radical enablers of change in the history of mankind, the integrated circuit and the Internet, are altering every aspect of civilization with astonishing speed.

The current crisis is an opportunity to take stock of our lives. Circumstances may also require us to simplify our personal lives. Christopher Nyerges's interest in wild foods, survival skills, and urban self-reliance has always been a practical—as well as a spiritual—quest to live lightly on the land. Most of the people in the world are now city dwellers; this book's emphasis on urban self-reliance therefore makes perfect sense. I have never reached anywhere near the level of self-reliance that Christopher and Dolores have, but I can wholeheartedly attest to the fact that even the tiniest adjustments can fill one with much satisfaction and help us regain in small increments a sense of purpose that is so chronically undermined by our consumer society. Every backyard vegetable bed, compost heap, or chicken coop, every home-grown kilowatt or normalized BTU, becomes an invitation to restore meaning to our lives.

Reflecting the urgency of our current predicament, this book puts more emphasis on the practical aspects of self-reliance than many of Christopher's previous books. It forms a comprehensive guide of the current technology and know-how that is available for self-reliance in the city. I highly recommend it to people seeking to better themselves and their daily lives.

—Carel Struycken

actor and permaculture advocate

Introduction

As energy costs continue to rise, more and more people are beginning to favor "self-reliance." In the 1960s, one of the triggers for the back-to-the-earth movement was the perception that society had lost its roots and individuals had lost their sense of self-reliance. Many of the back-to-the-earth folks were driven by a commitment to the environment. They were concerned that modern lifestyles were ruining the earth. They wanted to be a part of the solution. Economics were not the driving force in their decisions to grow their own food or produce some of their power.

As long as society functions smoothly overall, there are few worries. But when one part of the complex machine weakens or fails, we find that our lifestyles are threatened. When trash collectors in urban areas go on strike, garbage builds up on city streets, followed by foul odors, rats, and roaches. When truckers strike, food dwindles on supermarket shelves.

The whims of nature also affect our well-being, especially if we have no degree of self-reliance. Floods, earthquakes, fires, hurricanes, and other natural disasters all seem to conspire to tear apart our neat and tidy lives.

It's important to learn how to deal with one's own needs within the context of any household and also within the context of one's neighborhood. Learning and practicing skills of self-reliance makes good sense from ethical, moral, and spiritual perspectives as well as from ecological and economical standpoints. Self-reliance is vital for our personal and national survival.

We will explore the many ways in which a person can voluntarily go "off the grid," wholly or partly. We will also look at the many aspects of the quiet revolution that has been occurring, and we'll examine the details

NOTE

I strongly recommend that you also read my *Extreme Simplicity: Homesteading in the City* (with Dolores Nyerges) in which we describe many of the systems (including gardening and permaculture) that we put into practice. You should also check out my *How to Survive Anywhere*, as it includes practical ways to subsist in either the wilderness or the city.

of how many people have taken action for themselves without waiting for the government to do something.

Specifically, we'll look at how you can create some of your own electricity and use gas alternatives such as solar water heaters. We'll look at compost toilets for those who don't want to be a part of the sewer system, either by necessity of where they live or because of their remote location. You'll learn about people who collect and purify their own water from the rain and others who are powering their cars with vegetable oil instead of gas. We'll also look at those who grow all or some of their food. These— and more—are some of the ways in which you can choose to be self-reliant.

Individuals in modern society cannot be 100 percent self-sufficient. It is somewhat impractical—if not impossible—for the average person to construct every single element for every single project. You can't make photovoltaic cells in your garage, for example. Perhaps ironically, it is the very complexity of our specialized society that has created the possibility of some degree of personal self-reliance.

We live in a complex society with high degrees of specialization. You will remain a part of that system as you pursue self-reliance as outlined in this book. You'll be interacting with the system in a different mode, however, by supporting those industries that allow for as much individual autonomy as is possible in an urban environment.

Recall the long gasoline lines in the United States in 1973–1974 that were a result of the Arab oil embargo. There was much talk at that time about how we can and should be self-reliant as individuals and as a nation. But have we really moved down the path of self-reliance? Are we slow

learners, or are we disinclined to pursue ecological ventures until we have
run out of other options?

Every household in the United States should have solar modules on the
roof to produce all or some of its electrical needs. So why don't we? What
forces and entities stand to gain—or lose—if the country moves in that
direction?

President Jimmy Carter had some solar panels installed on the White
House roof as a symbolic gesture that he supported the solar industry. But
President Ronald Reagan had the panels removed when he took over the
office, stating that solar electricity was impractical. And, unfortunately,
many political leaders have continued to voice the objection that solar
electricity is not cost-effective, windmills are pipe dreams, and electric
cars are fantasies. These political leaders often tell us that we have no
other option than to continue our increasing reliance on foreign oil,
despite evidence to the contrary.

So the quiet revolution continues. A small but growing number of people
are moving ahead with some degree of energy self-reliance. They know it
makes sense ecologically, economically, and in case of emergencies. The
people who share their stories in this book are not listening to the
politicians.

Many people have told me that they want to install more alternate
energy devices but are not financially able to do so. However, everyone I
interviewed who built an energy-saving system reported that their systems
eventually paid for themselves. That is, over time, if you add up the savings from your gas, water, or electric bills, those savings will exceed the
cost of your system. That means you are doing good for yourself and for
the world in an economically viable manner.

So despite the clamoring voice of nearly every leading politician in the
United States, these individuals who saw the value of energy self-reliance
went ahead and proved the politicians wrong. These new pioneers—many
of whom were interviewed for this book—have proven that home-based
energy production is economically viable.

Many of the systems or devices mentioned in this book can be easily
purchased and are simple to install. Some require the do-it-yourself mindset of one who likes to work on things and solve problems. Some may be
more involved, but none are beyond the abilities of an average plumber or

electrician. All solar water heating systems involve plumbing, and all solar electrical systems involve electrical knowledge. I am a firm believer in hiring knowledgeable people to install, or help you install, your systems. Work with them, watch what they do, and ask lots of questions. That's how you learn.

I am neither exceptionally bright nor endowed with a bottomless pocketbook. Therefore, if I can do it, you can do it. Most of the people mentioned in this book are like you and me—people who wanted to do what is right and then simply moved forward.

This book is dedicated to those who do not wait for someone else to tell them what to do. This book is devoted to that enthusiastic, cooperative, pioneering spirit that will ultimately save us all.

In this book, you will learn about the following topics:
- Natural principles of cooling and heating a home
- Generation of electricity from the sun and wind
- Production of solar hot water
- Home rain collection (and other water issues)
- Alternatives to flush toilets
- Alternate transportation and fuels
- Permaculture

There are many other aspects of home self-reliance that are only dealt with here in passing. See the resources section at the end of this book for sources of information on these and other aspects of self-reliance.

1

DEVELOPING
A STRATEGY

So you're all excited about becoming self-reliant and you're eager to learn what it takes to get off the grid. Before you rush out and buy solar panels, however, let's first determine what it really takes to live your life ecologically and economically. Think about how you'd get by if an earthquake suddenly altered your normal day-to-day urban life. A lot of what you normally depend on would be gone, altered, or reduced. Does life require electricity? How would you meet your basic needs?

ONE MAN'S STORY

In 1965, Dude McLean and his young family moved into a house in Kagel Canyon, located in the hilly northern section of Los Angeles County. Kagel Canyon is nestled right up to the Angeles National Forest, a small canyon community of about two hundred families. He liked the house because there was a stream behind it that flowed year-round. "It was in the L.A. area, but I always felt distant from the L.A. craziness," says McLean. "My children barely realized that they were growing up near L.A."

Food Production

McLean, a former U.S. Marine, wanted a place where he could be as self-reliant as possible, even though his property didn't have a lot of land. He began doing French-intensive gardening, which requires a lot of digging, and then switched to square-foot gardening and raised beds. He grew carrots, kale, corn, beans, squash, and more in his garden. "We grew 90 percent of our own produce," says McLean. He learned how to garden by doing lots of reading and lots of experimenting. "Most of the work of

A productive urban garden.

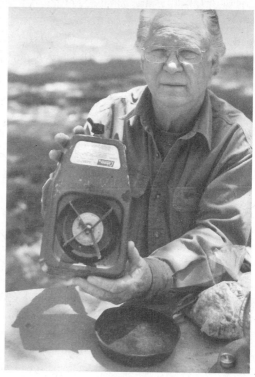

A single-burner Coleman stove that uses propane. "One tank, on a single burner, lasts me a week," says McLean.

gardening and producing your own food is in the preparation stages," explains McLean, who brought in horse and chicken manure and lots of mulch. "After two years, I could shove my arm into my garden soil and it would go in all the way up to my elbow." Once his garden was established, he could water it well in the summer and then go away for two weeks. Upon returning, the garden would be fine, even when it was very hot and dry. Although he grew no fruit trees, he was glad to have produced an environment that could feed his family.

Other Supplies
McLean wanted to be self-reliant in areas other than food production, so he began to build up the family's supply of camping gear. "I already had a pickup truck with a camper on it, and I began to purchase camping gear such as Coleman stoves, lanterns, sleeping bags, an ice chest, and even a porta-potty. And we always purchased used gear, if possible," he says. McLean explains that his family frequently went camping, so the entire family was well-versed in what it took to live well in the field.

Lighting
Since his canyon home was somewhat remote, it would lose electrical power for various reasons. McLean purchased kerosene lamps for the home and eventually had thirty-five gallons of kerosene fuel stored. He believed the kerosene lanterns would ensure more reliable long-term lighting than would battery-operated lanterns. "Batteries can fail," he says. "Well, you can also run out of kerosene, but I felt that the kerosene was a better choice."

He continued to obtain kerosene lanterns (he eventually had six), extra tents, and blankets, all of which were spaced out in the house, garage, and camper. His fully equipped camper had been customized with dual gas tanks and had a range of about eight hundred miles.

Part of what motivated McLean to become more self-reliant were the stories he'd heard from his grandmother about living through the great San Francisco earthquake of 1908. He grew up in Burbank and had been through some earthquakes as a teenager. But he says that the potential threat of a USSR–USA nuclear exchange during the Cold War was a strong motivating factor in his home preparedness.

McLean with some basic camping gear, all of which he used in the aftermath of the Sylmar earthquake.

A Dietz kerosene lamp burns with usable light for about twenty hours.

Water

"We had our own water supply in the canyon, supplied by artesian wells, but it always bothered me that the water supply could be interrupted for various reasons. So I always liked that we had a stream behind the house," says McLean.

Still, he began to store water. He obtained two forty-gallon barrels and started to store water in used glass soda bottles, his goal being to have at least two weeks' worth of water for the entire family. He eventually obtained ten large, glass Sparkletts Water bottles for water storage.

He had a good storage area in his garage but realized that in the event of an earthquake or hurricane, his home could be burned or destroyed, and he might not be able to readily get to his stored supplies. So he stored

Mclean used a collapsible, flax-fabric water container after the earthquake.

his water in different locations, putting some out in the yard and some in the garage. He also collected rainwater when he could.

Food

"We began to experiment with drying our own food on old window screens. We put the sliced food on the screens and put another screen on top to keep off the flies. Some of these experiments didn't work out, but mostly they did, and we stored a lot of what we dried," explains McLean.

He then began to store canned goods, such as meats, fruits, vegetables, and other nonperishable food items. "You have to remember that we never had any extra money," he says. "I couldn't go out and just buy a lot of stuff even if I wanted to. I had children and was self-employed. I would just spend a few extra dollars each time I went shopping and store a little more food. I never went out and made some big purchase. It was all done little by little, and I often purchased canned items when they were on sale."

The only foods purchased in bulk were beans, rice, and red winter wheat. He purchased a crank grinder and would grind wheat as needed for his family's bread and other pastry items. Within the first five years, he

Some types of dried provisions that McLean stored in his household.

learned to label all his stored items so that he would always use the oldest items first.

The Test

Then in 1971, when he and his wife were both 33, and his children were 2, 9, and 12, the 7.1 Sylmar earthquake hit. "As the crow flies, we were only about 5 miles from the epicenter of this quake," explains McLean.

It was early in the morning, about 5 A.M. "The noise of the quake was deafening. I can't even describe it. It was like being next to a train going by and you can't hear your conversation, but multiply that by a thousand," McLean recalls. "The earth was grinding and moving, and it was like a giant shock wave hit the house. It was like some giant had wrapped his hands around the house and shook it every which way. It was very much like being hit with a bomb. My first words when the quake began was 'They got us,' thinking we were hit by a Russian bomb."

But he then realized it was an earthquake. There was crashing in his house as things were falling everywhere, and he ran into the bedroom of his two youngest children. While the house was still shaking, he held one under each arm and carried them out of the house to a big field across the street.

"The house had four doors as exits, but I could only get one open because the others were jammed. So I took the two youngest to the field, set them down, and told them to stay. Then I ran back into the house, naked and barefoot, and got my older daughter out of the house." McLean took her to the field across the street with the other children and then went back to the house.

"My wife was turning in circles in the house," says McLean. As he explains it, all the walls were lined with plates and bookshelves, and everything was being tossed into the center of the room, falling over and breaking. In the kitchen, every cabinet had emptied onto the floor, which was littered with broken glass.

"I don't know how I escaped without getting my feet cut," says McLean, "but I just grabbed my wife, and we all went over to the field and stood there while everything was still shaking. Other neighbors started coming out and some came to the field. I could see that all the transformers on the telephone poles were down, and some houses up the creek had been thrown off their foundations and into the creek."

Damage Assessment

McLean explains that when it got light, neighbors checked on other neighbors, and there were no major injuries or deaths. The water line that provided water to the approximately two hundred homes in the canyon was broken every six to twenty feet, and telephone, electricity, and gas lines were out. The main access road to the canyon had shifted about two feet, so a truck was needed to get in or out.

About 30 percent of the homes in the canyon were totally destroyed. Some people packed up and never came back. About a dozen houses were shaken down to rubble piles about four feet high. Homes were down in the creek.

McLean's family didn't want to return to the house, but they went back to get clothes because it was cold. They eventually all sat in the truck and cooked some food on Coleman stoves for breakfast. Because the electricity was out, the family had no idea how bad the situation was beyond the canyon. They got through the first day by cleaning up the living room so they could use it as the bedroom that night. But when night came, no one wanted to sleep, so they all piled into the truck and drove out of the canyon to assess the damage.

They learned about the range of the quake's damage from scant news reports. The media focused on a collapsed hospital and the many bridges and overpasses that had collapsed. "I believe there was much more widespread damage," says McLean, "but we didn't have the freeway through here then, and we didn't have the instant media that we have now."

The family returned home and spent the first night there. The next day, McLean took his family to some relatives who lived in the high desert, then he returned to the house. He was only able to make it to the desert and back because of his familiarity with the old roads that were used before the freeway was constructed. Because so many bridges and overpasses had collapsed, it would have been impossible for him to take any main routes out of town.

The Cleanup

McLean worked on cleaning up the house by himself during the following week. He noted that it took four days for the government emergency services to get to the canyon to bring water supplies. It took three weeks for the regular water supply to be restored and at least that long for electricity to be restored. "The government can be very slow in reacting to emergencies, but we had plenty of supplies in food and water," he says. "I had a porta-potty, and I could bury the contents in the yard when full. But our toilet was actually on a septic system that still worked if I poured water into the bowl." He had a total of 120 gallons of stored water, some in glass containers that hadn't broken because they were packed well.

"I took short baths with just a little water. I cooked on the Coleman stoves with the food we'd stored. Plus, I didn't just take care of myself. I shared food and water with neighbors. I showed neighbors how to get water from the creek and boil it. It's still amazing to me that some people didn't know to do this. In general, everyone helped those who needed help. Perhaps the best thing we had going for us was that most of the neighbors knew each other. We had a community center at the park, and there were regular activities there for teens and adults. Knowing your neighbors is probably the best way to prepare for emergencies besides storing things and learning skills."

McLean's family came back a week after the earthquake hit, and everyone slept together in the living room. Gas lines were out, so they cut their own firewood using hand saws. They walked up the canyon and cut dead oak and sycamore branches to burn in their living room fireplace. Eventually, little by little, the utilities were restored and life went back to normal.

"After the quake, I remember thinking, 'Wow, I did the right thing.' Here I was preparing maybe for war, for the Russians to bomb us, or maybe for unemployment, but not for an earthquake like this. And I was very happy to be prepared," says McLean. "To this day, my son still vividly recalls that earthquake. That experience spurred me on to do even more extensive preparations. A disaster can be a job loss, a fire, anything. It's important to know what to store, where to store things, and how to store them."

McLean continued to study self-reliance and survival skills and built up an extensive research library of more than six hundred books. "But all the books in the world are no good if you don't put the information into practice," he adds. "I got to the point where I had a whole room in storage, and if I didn't have to go to the store for two years, I could have done that.

After the earthquake, McLean added hot water and oatmeal to this wide-mouth Thermos. The family then had hot oatmeal ready for breakfast.

We could have lived off the grid for two years, and I had backup systems for my backups," he laughs. McLean also advised many individuals and groups on how to prepare for emergencies and live self-reliantly, and he was very busy during the panic that accompanied the Y2K fears in 1999.

Advice

According to McLean, "The most basic thing for people to do is to have at least a few weeks of food and water. Plan at least a gallon of water per person per day. And don't store everything in one place, since you may not be able to get to your gear. Think through all your daily needs, make a list, and begin to get your supplies for sleeping, shelter, eating, cooking, lighting—everything."

With the pride of a father, he points out that all three of his children are now very self-reliant because they were raised that way, knowing how to camp and deal with the needs of everyday life. "Remember, I had to learn all this little by little, and we experimented," he says. "Sure, we were also preparing for possible emergencies, but we all had a great time doing it."

2

DEALING WITH
THE HEAT AND COLD

Now that you've learned the importance of being somewhat self-reliant, especially in an emergency, let's look at your home and find all the ways you can make it more efficient using natural principles. These natural forces can be tapped in order to stay cooler inside when it's scorching hot outside and warmer indoors when it's freezing outdoors. Part of our ability to tap these natural forces has much to do with how well the house was planned, aligned in its particular terrain, and built. Unfortunately, for most of us, we're living in a house built decades ago with no regard to sun and wind alignment or to ecological and economical living. So we end up trying to do the best we can with what we have and find ways to make the best of a bad situation.

STAYING COOL

We are constantly assaulted by the forces of nature, especially in the form of heat, cold, wind, rain, storms, and other weather phenomena. How the masses of hot air and cold air come together and create such weather is fascinating, and you'd benefit by learning more about it in a book such as Eric Sloane's *Weather Book*. But let's try to stick with the basics by reviewing some of the many principles that enable us to stay cool.

Part of the problem with constantly changing weather is that people have settled down in their homes and cities and have no desire to move nomadically with the seasons. Plus, the country's population is too great to be able to do that. We therefore deal with the conditions of weather no matter where we are.

Before addressing specific details in regards to your house, let's take a moment and look at our own bodies and how they're designed to help us stay cool. When it's hot, we sweat, which helps cool us down a bit. Yet in our modern world, people are extremely worried about the fact that our bodies are designed to sweat. There is a million-dollar industry designed to make us smell good because we sweat. Any drugs or surgery designed to prevent the body from sweating, however, are *not* good ideas and are ultimately bad for the health of the body. The body is designed to sweat for a reason. The pores not only excrete water to help cool us down, but they also excrete toxins.

Liquids

As we sweat, we lose water, causing us to drink more fluids. Some fluids actually lead to a greater net loss than a net gain. For example, alcohol and caffeinated beverages replenish the water the body is losing, but the increase in perspiration and urination becomes greater than what is retained. Research has also shown that adding a little bit of raw apple cider vinegar to drinking water or fruit juice will enable you to deal with the heat just a little better.

During the late 1970s, when I first learned of this through the WTI Survival Training School, I would routinely add from one teaspoon to one tablespoon of raw apple cider vinegar to each quart of water or fruit juice I drank. After working in the heat, I found that I was far less exhausted when I'd added the vinegar to the water than when I did not. I have experienced this enough times to know that it was not merely psychosomatic. Plus, I have experienced the added bonus of mosquitoes leaving me alone when they are biting everyone else. The vinegar apparently affects one's body chemistry and causes mosquitoes to stay away.

Clothing

During times of heat, you need to adjust your clothing accordingly. This should be easy enough to do when at home, as you ought to have both a summer and winter wardrobe. Summer clothes should be loose-fitting and made of a lightweight fabric such as cotton or other natural fiber. Polyesters do not breathe as well as cottons.

People who live their lives in the desert wear loose-fitting robes. Note how different that is from the average American who gets a free weekend and travels to the beach wearing the skimpiest of outfits. This is fine if you want to show off, but it's not great for your body's health.

Once, while leading a group on a wilderness class in the heat of the summer, two hikers came by dressed in shorts and tank tops. The woman says to me, "Why are you dressed like that?" I was wearing long khaki pants, a light cotton khaki shirt, and a wide-brimmed hat. I was very comfortable and wanted to stay that way. Before I could answer, they ambled off into the wild blue yonder.

Later in the day, as I was still hydrated and feeling good, they passed us again as they were heading up the hill to their car. They looked tired and haggard, and their skin was brilliant pink. "Do any of you know what poison oak looks like?" she asked, but didn't wait around for an answer. She and her companion simply continued on the trail, dragging their feet and kicking up dust.

"Do you see what I see?" I asked my students. We then had a brief discussion about how the hiking couple went into the heat overexposed and consequently lost moisture. They got scratched up, sun-burned, and almost suffered heat stroke. They probably walked through the ubiquitous poison oak wearing short pants. My long pants and shirt, loose-fitting and light-weight, protected me from all that. As it was a very hot day, my students and I would also occasionally wet our clothes to create wearable "swamp coolers."

Diet
You should also keep your diet in mind when temperatures rise. Heavy, starch-laden foods require more water to digest and are best avoided. Salads, fruits, organic fruit drinks, vegetables, and lighter foods cause less stress to your body in times of heat. It is no great mystery that watermelon is a favorite food in summer!

COOLING YOUR HOME
The above suggestions represent ways you can make your body less vulnerable to the heat. Now let's get to your house and yard.

Let's first assume that you did *not* build your home so that you get the best solar exposure in winter and the least in summer, and you did *not* landscape your yard to take advantage of the local geology and wind flow. Let's assume you are like more than 90 percent of the city-dwelling people who simply purchased or rented a place and now have to make the best of the situation.

I have been in that situation numerous times—sometimes the house was ideally suited to taking advantage of nature's forces and sometimes it was not. In my Highland Park home, it was unbearably hot every summer. The house was built in a low pocket in a valley, and there seemed to be no wind flow through the area. It was neither ideally suited to take advantage of the sun in the winter nor to take advantage of natural cooling in the summer. Out of desperation, we went to Sears and purchased a window air conditioner. This was some twenty years ago and we knew nothing about the Energy Star program. The air conditioner kept the house temperature tolerable during those ten to twenty days a year when the outside temperature was completely unbearable. It also sucked up electricity and drove up the bill.

White Roof

Coincidentally, the roof on our Highland Park home was no good and we needed a new one. I knew that sooner or later we'd need to bite the bullet and reroof the entire place. My natural instinct to save money and put off the roofing project as long as possible led me to find a short-term alternative—a white liquid rubber product that I painted over the existing roof like thick paint. (There are several such products at home improvement stores; the last one I purchased was Henry's Solarflex 287.)

My primary intent was to seal all the leaks in the bad roof until I could afford to hire roofers. I wasn't happy that the product was brilliant white. I then learned that—besides sealing small leaks—this product was also marketed to those who live in trailers and mobile homes with metal roofs that get hot. Once the roof was sealed in this white rubber product, we found that the inside temperature during the summer was about 15 degrees cooler. This was a significant difference, and it meant that the air conditioner was now on maybe three to four days a year, not ten to twenty.

A white roof stays cooler during the summer and can keep inside temperatures 15 degrees cooler than with a dark roof.

I used this white rubber product on my current roof in Altadena and found that the inside temperature during the day was at least 15 degrees cooler, all a result of the reflective qualities of white. I would strongly recommend this product to anyone. Similarly, when reroofing your home, you should always insist on the whitest possible shingles.

Attic Space

Once, when my friend Eric Zammit was visiting, we got to talking about natural methods of cooling one's home. I told him that I wanted to insulate my attic but had not yet done so because I wanted to tear out the ceiling and create a much larger inside space. Eric said that he had a similar problem in his home and that I would be better off not to take out my ceiling. Even without insulation, Eric said, the space between the ceiling and the roof traps heat and actually serves as a buffer to keep the house cooler. So I never removed the ceiling.

Attic Fan

After talking with Eric, I went up into the attic on a hot day and realized it was *very* hot up there—perhaps as much as 20 degrees hotter than it was down in the living room. Of course, that's partly because heat rises, but also because the sun was beating down on the roof. What else could be done to make the inside of the house cooler that wouldn't cost a lot?

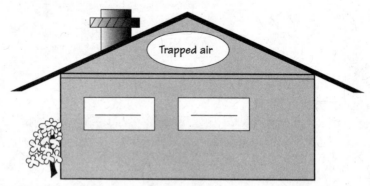

The attic space traps air and acts as an insulating buffer, even if you have no insulation in your ceiling. A ceiling between the room and the roof will thus keep your room slightly cooler.

I had my friend Wade Webb come over and look at a used solar panel I had in the garage. (He had previously installed our small solar electric system.) I showed Wade the solar panel, the surface of which was cracked, that someone had thrown into a trash can at a convention hall. Wade tested it and said that it was still good. I epoxied a clear plastic sheet over the top surface so no water would get inside, then Wade worked another miracle on the roof.

He put a small 12-volt fan in the attic at one of the vents; this fan was then powered by the refurbished solar panel. He installed an on/off switch in a closet, which allowed us to turn on the fan during the summer but leave it off in the winter. By using the power of the sun, we were able to blow the heat out of the attic, dropping the attic heat by measurable degrees and making the house much more comfortable during the summer.

There are numerous commercial solar-powered attic fans to consider. One is the SolarStar attic fan, a one-piece unit with a solar module on top that sucks the hot air out of your attic. This unit has no on/off switch—it works whenever there is sun striking the module. It's simple and easy for any homeowner to install.

Insulation

Probably the most cost-effective single thing that a homeowner can do to keep cool in summer (and warm in winter) is to heavily insulate every wall in the house as well as the ceiling and floor space. Regardless of what method you then use to cool (or heat) your home, your heavy insulation will keep the house cool in summer and warm in winter.

There are lots of ways to insulate walls and wall spaces, such as with foam that can be blown through a little hole so you don't need to rip out the walls in order to insulate your home. Obviously, it would have been better if this was done as the house was being built, but if it wasn't, you can still insulate little by little, beginning with the rooms that you use the most.

Part of the insulation process is to get double-walled windows, which contain at least two panes of glass that provide an insulating air pocket, thus cutting down on heat or cold loss by means of convection.

In some climates, heavy insulation could reduce your use of a cooler or heater or even eliminate the need to purchase a costly air conditioner or heating system altogether.

Morgan Hartley shows the top view of a commercial solar attic fan sold by Phat Energy.

The fan, underneath, is directly powered by the solar panel on top.

Keep in mind that each of these measures helped just a little and the costs—sealing the roof, insulating empty space, and cooling the attic—were starting to add up. We wondered whether we could get things any cooler using just natural principles.

AIR CIRCULATION

One of the problems with our Highland Park house was that it was located in a low area with very little air circulation. The inside of the house remained very hot during the summer, even at night. We knew that we'd have better air circulation if we opened certain windows, which helped to a certain extent. But the north-to-south airflow was blocked by the rear and front door, and we were hesitant to leave the doors open all night with just flimsy screen doors for protection. We therefore installed some iron security screen doors on the front and rear, which allowed us to keep the front and rear doors open all night and get the airflow that kept the temperature very comfortable—never muggy and stuffy.

Airflow

While visiting some friends in Highland Park many years ago on a hot summer day, I noted they had no air conditioning or fans and certainly no central air. It was a hundred-year-old house, built before electricity was the norm. It was not cold—or even cool—in their living room, as is often the case when you enter modern stores and offices in summer. But it was definitely comfortable and far cooler than the stifling 100-plus degrees heat outside. What had they done?

The living room was approximately 25 by 10 feet, with the long side facing south, and it had two large windows. There was a door on the east and a window on the west. The large picture windows were covered with white sheets, which admitted light but kept out much of the brightness and heat of the sun. Both the east door and west window were open, and both were covered in a wet sheet, which was periodically replaced. (As I recall, they put some towels underneath the sheets to catch the excess water.) The air was cooled by the moisture in the sheets, creating a cool breeze through the room.

Ancient Egyptians invented the first evaporative coolers (also known as "swamp coolers") when they hung camel-hair rugs soaked in water over the doorways and windows of their living spaces.

Airflow is important, so you should make a point of observing your local airflows. I have cooled my home at night simply by opening doors—a no-brainer. But some houses have a more complicated airflow pattern, so you need to take the time to observe the patterns in your home.

HEAT RISES

One way a large two-story house can be kept cool in the summer is by opening the windows on the northern shady side and the cooler east side, and opening one upper window just a crack in the upstairs west side. Imagine the hot air rising in the house, flowing out that western crack but bringing with it a slight airflow of the cooler air from the cooler sides of the house.

Jared Anderson lives in a tepee in the shadow of downtown Los Angeles.

This may seem like a little thing—and perhaps it is—but it is one of the many little things that enable you to live in relative comfort without using any resources at all. It allows you to live with nature's principles.

Back when tepees dominated the flatlands, Native Americans also utilized natural airflow. On very hot days on the Plains, the bottom part of the tepee canvas would be rolled up a foot or so to leave an open space all around the bottom. Hot air rising in a narrower space (such as in the cone shape of the tepee) will speed up just slightly as the air exits the smoke flap. This is known as the Venturi effect, and it allowed Native Americans to have a type of air conditioning without electricity.

There are more simple ways to cut down the heat in one's home, although these methods are not always easy to implement. If you live in the desert, for example, your home is constantly assaulted by the heat. Trees and a white roof help, but some enterprising desert dwellers have also built what amounts to massive canopies over their homes. Large vertical posts are secured around the house, and a "roof" of sheet metal is installed. This creates a buffer between the heat of the sun and the roof of the house. This is akin to the attic space in the house that provides some insulating space, thereby keeping the home cooler.

Another large-scale innovation, also done on desert homes, is to create a large flat roof over which canvas is secured. Water is then run down over the roof from the top and absorbed by the fabric before it evaporates. In essence, this method is like having a large swamp cooler over one's home. This method has been documented on Hugh Howser's public television programs, although I don't know whether it's still being employed in today's desert homes.

FORBES'S ADVICE

I spoke with alternate energy innovator Glenn Forbes, who shared some commonsense suggestions for natural cooling and heating. He states, "If you are expecting hot days, open the windows all night long to remove any heat buildup. Do the reverse for heating. Shade trees around your home are good, too. Also consider misters to cool things off. If the humidity is low, swamp coolers work well."

One of the objections that many people have to opening the windows at night is fear of intruders. Indeed, many burglars have gained access to homes when the windows were open for precisely this reason. Before I moved into my Altadena home, all the windows had security bars, and there were security screen doors. The owner offered to remove them, thinking that I would find them unsightly. I asked him to leave them, which has allowed me to keep doors and windows open day and night as needed and not worry about anyone invading my home.

STEVE LAMB'S ADVICE

I spoke with Altadena resident and architect Steve Lamb about how to increase the cooling and heating efficiency of our homes. According to Lamb, "The first and perhaps most important thing you can do to make a house naturally energy efficient is to properly site the home. You want natural early morning light from high windows in the bedrooms, meaning that you want your bedrooms on the east. You want most of your solar heat gain from the south, and you want to reduce your western late afternoon heat gain in the summer but use it in the winter. The latter can be accomplished by planting deciduous trees that drop leaves in winter and shade in summer. Shading your bedroom with trees during the summer is also a smart thing to do. My 1906 single-wall (1-inch-thick redwood walls) house follows these strategies and is comfortable year-round.

"In the Southern California climate, you want as much shading roof overhang as you can get. If you think three feet is good, go to five feet. This creates a cooler microclimate around the house and keeps your wall areas from heating up. You can do what Frank Lloyd Wright did and open the rafters at the points where you want solar heat gain.

"My studio was rebuilt after a fire and has modern insulation in it. I deepened the south overhangs from the one foot they had before the fire to a full five feet. This cooled things down a lot, as did the R-30 fiberglass batt insulation in the roof and the R-19 in the walls. I wanted to use spray-in polyurethane insulation, but our retrograde county won't let you do that yet. If I had, the ceiling would have been R-75 and the walls R-35. Some people are afraid of polyurethane and some are allergic. Cork insulates just as well and doesn't emit any poisonous gases, which can't be said of polyurethane and most man-made rigid insulation panels. It was approved up until the 1950s, but it isn't approved now due to bogus fire concerns—

Architect Steve Lamb in front of a Pasadena residence he modified to make more energy-efficient, such as adding larger overhangs to provide more shade.

have you ever tried to start cork on fire? It's a *lot* of work. Still, cork is heavy and expensive.

"I have G.E. thermoclear skylights that I designed. They provide natural sunlight all day long, don't leak water, don't generate too much heat gain, and would produce less heat gain had I used a thicker lens.

"But again, one of the best things about my studio was the neighbor's eucalyptus tree that shaded it all year long. A couple of years ago, he cut it down and that *really* decreased the comfort. It also took away the wonderful dappled light that used to dance across my skylight."

Size

Lamb also had some key ideas on how to plan efficiency into a building. "Most people think they need too many rooms and that they need them too big," he says. "I have been in some gigantic homes that were no more comfortable or expansive to the mind than a shoebox. I have seen small homes with well-planned vistas and a sense of openness that made you feel you were in the most open expansive place imaginable.

"A 12 by 24 by 8 room means 2,128 cubic feet to heat and cool. A room with the same or even lower function that is 16 by 36 by 12 means 6,876 cubic feet to heat and cool. It's double the square feet but triple the cubic feet. Worse yet, the larger the mass of air to heat and cool, the more difficult it is to heat, cool, and keep at temperature, and the more detrimental the air leaks become. So whatever you can do to reduce the volume of the rooms and still keep open sight lines for the psychological benefit of the inhabitants is vital. The *worst* thing you can do is construct a tall, vertical room. That's just throwing heating and cooling money down the sewer. The

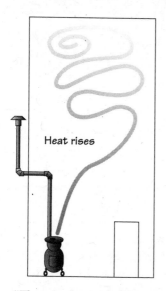

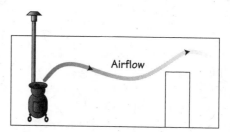

**VERTICAL ROOM
(high ceiling)
vs.
HORIZONTAL ROOM
(low ceiling)**

Heat rises

Airflow

"The more horizontal a room, the more its tendency to transfer the warm or cool air across to the inhabitants. The more vertical, the more the tendency to transfer the warm or cool air up and away from the inhabitants. Vertical rooms also can lead to inversion layers where the hot air rises and forces the cool air down, which is not desirable in winter."

—Steve Lamb

Traditional, adobe-style homes with thick walls stay cooler naturally in the summer.

more horizontal a room, the more its tendency to transfer the warm or cool air across to the inhabitants. The more vertical, the more the tendency to transfer the hot or cool air up and away from the inhabitants. Vertical rooms can also lead to inversion layers where the hot air rises and forces the cool air down, which is not desirable in winter.

"Having said that, high, well-insulated windows that are directly under the eaves and don't really have views are excellent devices for taking heat off the ceiling in the summer and causing drafts for cooling. You could make some out of plywood-and-cork sandwich—cork being the best natural insulator—but nowadays the code requires any hinged opening device to be made by an approved manufacturer. Until someone starts making them in a factory, we're stuck with less-efficient windows.

"None of these ideas are new. They were common folk knowledge, and they were found in the works of some Arts and Crafts architects such as Frank Lloyd Wright, early Greene and Greenes, all of Louis B. Easton's work, and even by Richard Neutra in his work before World War II.

"A book that has some of the best ideas in it and that is still ahead of the times in what it demonstrates as being available options is *Shelter* by Ten

Note the porch overhang, which provides shade and natural cooling, on this traditional adobe house.

The Greene and Greene Gamble House in Pasadena, California.

Another view of the Gamble House.

Note the large, cooling roof overhang.

Speed Press, first published in the 1970s. Many of the ideas in there are still just as useful, practical, and more time-proven than ever but are still not allowed under our codes, even as the codes become more allegedly 'green.'

"A lot of this green crap that is being approved is high maintenance and high tech, and it has high poison content in its manufacture. It's corporate nonsense that finds a way to mitigate a poorly designed and sited building, or a way to get extra LEED points by doing cutie-pie things like constantly adjusting the lighting in an inhabited room for maximum efficiency, not of course taking into account the actual and psychological needs of the user in the room. I, for example, find it annoying when someone else is jiggering my lights. There are lenses that can be used easily, cheaply, and permanently to throw light throughout a room, but you can't get any LEED points for using that hundred-year-old technology!"

HEAT PUMPS

Heat pumps can be used for both heating and cooling. They work by extracting warmth and coolness either from the outside air or the ground. According to the August 2008 issue of *Scientific American*, "heat pumps can provide greater efficiency and lower cost over the long haul. . . . They can attain greater efficiency than conventional designs because instead of consuming fuel to generate warmth or coolness from scratch, they exploit heat or cold already present in the outside air or ground."

Heat pumps circulate this heat or cold via electricity; they are therefore considered the most efficient form of electric heat. They are essentially air conditioners with a switch, so they can be used for either cooling or heating. Heat pumps are best used in climates with colder winters or where natural gas is not available. One air-conditioning serviceman I spoke with said that the initial cost is high, and although heat pumps are more efficient over time, they do not heat as well as gas furnaces. This was his explanation as to why heat pumps still constitute only a small portion of the air-conditioning market.

HOW TO STAY WARM

Some of the principles for keeping your place warm when it's cold outside have already been addressed. Let's begin with what you need to do and wear to stay warm; we'll then discuss how to keep your home warm when the temperature drops.

Keep in mind that we're all different and have different tolerances to temperature variations. Up to a point, I like the cold. I like the doors and windows wide open, especially when it's raining outside. I like the feel of the breeze and the coolness of the air. There is something mentally and spiritually refreshing when the cool breezes pass through my room. But how many times have I heard others say, "Can you please close the door? I'm freezing"? Sometimes they say it politely, and sometimes with great anger.

I have my limits, of course. When I lived in Ohio with my brother, the winter temperature was once below zero for weeks. We had an oil furnace then, and it was expensive to heat the farmhouse without a woodstove, so we blocked off the other rooms of the house and just heated the kitchen, bedroom, and the living room on occasion. One sunny winter day, the temperatures got up to 40 degrees F, and people in the town square were walking around in T-shirts saying there was a heat wave. I was still in my coat, but it was clear how our body's limitations are all very different. Dealing with the cold, however, is not merely a state of mind. There are also practical measures that can be taken

For example, every pore of our body should be free of detritus to allow the body to excrete toxins. Our pores also help with our comfort level when it is hot or cold. So to keep my pores doing their job, I thoroughly scrub my skin when I take baths, using a stiff Fuller brush that was probably designed to clean a sink or toilet. (Someone with more sensitive skin should probably use a brush with softer bristles.)

I also drink warm fluids when it is very cold, despite the fact that this may mean that I go to the bathroom more often. You wouldn't need to tell a child to have a warm beverage or hot soup on a cold day, but I know adults who won't drink hot tea or coffee (or even hot water) because they don't want to have to go to the bathroom more often. In some very rare cases I can understand this, but usually, bathrooms are everywhere. We all have one in our homes, right? Consume warm beverages so you're more comfortable in the cold. Dress warmly. Exercise a bit during the day. Obviously, increasing cardiovascular activity will help warm the entire body.

Upon hearing this last piece of advice, someone once said to me, "You must be out of you mind! Should we be doing jumping jacks in the snow?" Yes, I know this may not be for everyone, but simple lifestyle changes and modifications can make all the difference in the world. After all, isn't it our modern lifestyles that have created many ecological and economical crises?

How long should we cling to the faulty logic of "I'm just doing what everyone else is doing" as an excuse to not change our behavior?

HEATING YOUR HOME

Once you've taken the necessary steps to keep yourself warm, you can move on to modifying your home. In terms of the greatest energy savings per dollar spent, insulating your walls, ceiling, and floor is by far the best investment. Before you concern yourself with exotic new appliances and fancy solar warmers, insulate!

Low-Tech Insulation

Fred Peters, a friend of my father's who grew up in Bedford Heights, Ohio, often told the story of how he insulated his home. In the 1920s and '30s, everyone heated their homes with furnaces, and a truck would deliver the fuel when needed. In the winter after snow had fallen, Fred noticed that the snow would always melt on the roofs of all the houses in his neighborhood. He reasoned that this was because all the heat from the furnace was melting the snow instead of heating the house.

At the time, Fred worked at a lumber mill as an after-school job, and during the following spring and summer, he managed to bring home a bag of wood shavings every day. He took each bag and packed it into the attic spaces between the rafters. By the following winter, he'd fully insulated his attic using this method. He never told his father about it because he felt his father would tell him not to do it.

As Fred came home each day the following winter, he noticed that the snow on his family's house lingered longer than any other roof in the neighborhood. He knew he had been right; by insulating the roof, he was keeping more of the heat in the house.

Fred still hadn't told his father. A few weeks into the winter, his father commented that it must be a mild winter because they still had plenty of fuel in the heater tank and hadn't needed to call the fuel delivery man as often. Fred finally took his father outside and asked him to look at all the neighboring roofs, including their own. His father was mystified as he noticed for the first time that their roof was still full of snow while all the others were snow-free.

"What's going on?" asked his father. Fred then told his father what he'd done, how he'd gotten permission from work to bring home a bag or two of chips each day, and how little by little he'd filled all the gaps in the attic.

"And your father was delighted, right?" I asked Fred.

"My father hit the roof. I can't tell you how angry he was," Fred said, and went on to explain that his father was mad because he was not in control. Within a week or so, however, Fred's father finally thanked and acknowledged him for what he'd done.

I never forgot this story from my father's friend about what he'd accomplished "in secret." Still, I wonder how safe flammable wood chips would have been in the attic—probably not very. Today's modern insulations, however, are largely fire-retardant and would not represent the same potential fire danger, or weight, as wood chips in the attic.

Modern Appliances

Replacing old appliances with modern models is another way to save money and conserve energy. Again, although the initial cost may be high, the long-term benefits to both your wallet and the environment will be well worth the investment. According to Glenn Forbes, high-quality appliances can even help heat your home. He offers the following advice: "For keeping heat inside in the winter, try to contain the heat to just the rooms you will be sleeping or cooking in by shutting the inside doors. Just by keeping the kitchen door closed, the heat from the refrigerator will warm up that room or the one connected to it." Refrigerators stay cool on the inside because heat is ejected outside via the coils typically found on the back of the refrigerator.

Energy Star

You might be ready to install another heating (or cooling) system, but it's important to do your homework before you make a purchase to determine what is most appropriate for your needs.

Your best choice for an over-the-counter system will be one with the Energy Star seal of approval. Energy Star is a joint program of the U.S. Environmental Protection Agency and the U.S. Department of Energy that helps us all "save money and protect the environment through energy efficient products and practices."

According to their Web site, "Results are already adding up. Americans, with the help of Energy Star, saved enough energy in 2007 alone to avoid greenhouse gas emissions equivalent to those from 27 million cars—all the while saving $16 billion on their utility bills."

Choosing energy-efficient appliances can save families about a third on their energy bill with similar savings of greenhouse gas emissions, without sacrificing features, style, or comfort.

- If looking for new household products, look for ones that have earned the Energy Star seal. They meet strict energy-efficiency guidelines set by the EPA and U.S. Department of Energy.
- If looking for a new home, look for one that has earned the Energy Star seal.
- If looking to make larger improvements to your home, the EPA offers tools and resources to help you plan and undertake projects to reduce your energy bills and improve home comfort. Visit their Web site at www.epa.gov.

Filters

In the central heating system in my father's house, there was a filter that had to be regularly cleaned or replaced. During the winter, my father would regularly be in the basement, shaking out the filter or putting in a new one. This was a simple enough task, and as a child, I wondered why he was always down there tinkering around. After all, I wasn't paying the bills—he was! Even though my father didn't carefully articulate the reason for it, he often had me or one of my brothers help him with this five-minute job of removing and cleaning the filter. The filter was washable and would get replaced maybe once a year. My father wasn't particularly concerned about saving energy, but with a family of six children, he was very concerned about saving money.

A clogged filter means that the heating (or cooling) delivery system is working harder and more inefficiently. Keeping *any and all* appliances working properly can be a big part of efficiently using our resources. This is especially true when heating and cooling a house.

Thermostats

Most people turn on the heat when they're cold and turn it off when they're warm; that's what we did in our home growing up. Modern technology, however, offers a better solution.

Programmable energy-saving thermostats allow you to only heat your home when you need to. They can be programmed to turn off when you're asleep, when you don't need as much heat. They can also be programmed to turn on the heat on very cold days just before you get home. Installing a programmable thermostat is a simple upgrade and an easy way to make your home more energy-efficient.

Off the Grid

Remember, the combined design of the house and the insulation of all the walls is the best way to keep your house cool in the summer and warm in the winter. In several places where I lived, I never used any sort of central heating. This was partly due to the design of the home and partly because I enjoy a home in winter that is a bit on the cool side. When it gets too cold, I'll put on a sweatshirt before resorting to a heat source.

Woodstoves and fireplaces are the obvious heating choices for anyone who doesn't want to use gas or electric heat. In most parts of the country, you can obtain firewood for free, usually year-round, merely by collecting and cutting it yourself. If uncertain as to whether you'd be trespassing or breaking any laws by collecting firewood, just ask the property owner.

I admit to having purchased firewood on occasion. By planning ahead, however, I've been able to bring home logs from trees that were being pruned or cut down (some already cut to woodstove or fireplace size) and stack them in the yard. You can also produce your own fuel from your yard (or neighborhood) by saving all the wood from tree prunings, cut to size and stacked to dry.

Woodstoves

There are many woodstoves from which to choose; whole books have been written on the possibilities, and it seems that every other issue of *Mother Earth News* mentions woodstoves. Before buying a woodstove, you should have an idea of where you want to place it. The location should heat as much of the house as possible, not just the corner of a room. The layout of your home may determine what sort of woodstove you will buy.

Although you can go to a fireplace store or catalog and buy any of the marvelous stoves available, I'd strongly suggest you begin by talking with friends who may already have a woodstove. Ask them why they selected their model, and find out the pros and cons of that model. After a while of doing this, you'll discover that there is no right or wrong woodstove; the choice simply depends on your particular situation and needs.

You should also start looking for woodstoves at flea markets and yard sales—you would be surprised how often you'll find these for sale, especially in certain parts of the country. When you see one, just start examining it and asking the owner questions. Is there significant rust? Is there burnout in certain areas? Do the doors open and close well? Are there pieces missing? Is it only good for heating, or can you also cook on the top? Will it fit in the spot you have in mind? Does it have sufficient height? Will it need to be put on a pedestal? Is it large enough to accommodate the size of firewood you have? Or will you need to cut the firewood into very small pieces? Will you need to buy the smoke pipes, or does the seller have them? Does the look of the stove appeal to you? The woodstove will become a central part of your home, and you want one that will provide you with years of service without being a nightmare.

Many woodstoves are entirely cast-iron, which means they get very hot. Some are made of sheet metal, and thus will not last as long. Some of the early Sears models were cast-iron internally, but then were coated in white enamel to look like a modern stove. Some are covered in layers of soapstone, which is an excellent choice because the stone will absorb and radiate heat for hours. You might pay more for a soapstone stove, but it's well worth it in the long run.

If you buy a used woodstove, you must examine it carefully inside and out and try to get a good deal. Remember, there are only a few reasons why someone would sell a woodstove. One, it might be a smoky stove with broken parts and the owner is tired of it. This might be fine for someone who wants an ornamental object in the yard, but not for someone who wants a workhorse. Two, it could be an estate sale in which someone died and all the furniture is being liquidated. Three, the stove might be fine, but the owner no longer wants to bring wood into the house and then deal with all the wood ash on a regular basis. A person with a self-reliant mindset feels good about doing these things, but there are many reasons why someone will choose to do otherwise (for example, an elderly person who is now living alone). Four, the city may have become hypnotized by political correctness and passed a law forbidding woodstoves—yes, that *is* actually a trend. Learn your local laws before you purchase the stove. Although many people are "green-friendly," the city authorities often have other ideas.

I have purchased new and used woodstoves and always felt that I got the better deal when I made a careful purchase of a used one. You can read all about the used woodstove that Dolores purchased and I installed in the book *Extreme Simplicity: Homesteading in the City,* which can be obtained used from Amazon.com or used bookstores (it is out of print).

Safety

Safety is of paramount importance. You don't want to burn your house down as a result of self-reliance. First, don't put a woodstove directly on a wood floor. You must lay down a safety layer of bricks or special boards used specifically for this purpose. The woodstove must not be any closer than 18 inches to the wall, although there are wall protectors designed to allow you to situate the stove a bit closer.

Typically, the smoke piping will go either 1) horizontally though the wall and then up vertically, 2) straight up vertically through the roof (where there is no ceiling), or 3) up through a ceiling and then through the roof, the latter of which is the most common. The method you use is determined entirely by your house configuration and where you decide to put your stove.

When I installed our woodstove, I could have used the third method since we had a ceiling in the living room. Rather than go straight up vertically, however, I connected the smoke pipe up nearly to the ceiling, then I put in a 90-degree elbow and ran the pipe about 5 feet horizontally. I then put in another elbow for the piping to go vertically through the ceiling and through the roof. This brought more heat into the room, rather than having most of the heat simply go out into the night.

There is a special triple-walled insulated device for where the pipe goes through the ceiling that you'll want to purchase, and then another special smokestack for where the pipe goes through the roof. Do not try to cut corners here; you don't want a super-hot pipe to touch the wood of your roof and burn down your house. When you feel everything is safely installed, first start a small fire and test to see if any smoke comes out of any of the pipes—this would mean you don't have a tight seal.

On a final safety note, if there are children in your household, you must find some way to create a barricade around the woodstove so that they don't get burned.

Fireplaces

In general, fireplaces are less efficient than woodstoves when it comes to heating your home. This is largely because most fireplaces are designed very simply, and most of the combustible gases end up going right out the chimney. The brick heats up somewhat, however, so there is some radiant heat from the bricks after the fire dies down.

The Russian fireplace is a design in which several baffles are built into the fireplace, slowing the combustible gases so that more heat is radiated into the house. This design is much more massive than a typical "ornamental" fireplace, and in some cases, the house is designed around it.

If you are living in a house where a standard fireplace was built, there are still things you can do to increase its efficiency. I once lived in a house with a fireplace at one end of a very long living room. If you were in the end of the room that had the fireplace, you'd be warm. But if you were on the other end of the room, you could actually still be cold. We added a grate composed of hollow tubes rather than just solid metal; the tubes then opened into the room. The idea was that the air in the space inside the tubes was heated and would naturally flow back into the room. The use of this grate increased the warming quality of the fireplace by perhaps 20 percent, which was significant. I have also seen such grates with hollow tubes combined with a fan that blows the hot air back into the room. This seems like a great idea, though I have never personally tried one.

Steve Lamb had the following to say about this topic: "Annoyingly, the state of California has just passed regulations against wood-burning fireplaces. The good news is that if your only heat comes from a wood-burning fireplace, you can use it. For real heat you need a *real masonry* fireplace. Those steel zero-clearance things may as well be a television set for all the actual warmth they produce. Real masonry is heated by the wood and stores the heat in the masonry mass and slowly releases it throughout the day. The best of these I have found are the soapstone units. They throw heat out for hours on end. A good hot fire early in the morning and one around dinnertime in a real masonry unit located near the physical center of the home will keep you warm in the coldest winter."

Solar Heaters

During visits to Ohio and Nebraska, I've seen solar heaters that measure approximately 4 feet by 8 feet by a few inches thick. They hang out the bottoms of south-facing windows. The sun heats air inside these boxes; the air then flows back into the room. The effectiveness of such solar heaters depends largely on the local conditions and the unit's alignment to the sun.

Some people I've met have really liked them, and others have told me that the result is negligible. When trying to retrofit an existing house and make it more energy-efficient, solar heaters might have their place.

Amish Building Practices

I was first exposed to the Amish when I lived in rural Ohio after graduating from high school. Years later, in the late 1990s, I was able to go inside many Amish homes and workplaces with Peter Gail, author of *Plain and Happy Living: Amish Recipes and Remedies*, who also conducts tours of the Amish countryside.

The Amish eschew nearly all modern conveniences, including electricity. They live in this world but are not of it. All Amish do not hold to identical beliefs about their use of appliances and modern devices, something that Peter once tried to explain to me. Each local leader can make decisions about such matters, and it often revolves around the issue of whether or not the appliance or device will more readily bring in the influences of modern society and whether or not such usage is "prideful."

Most Amish live in Ohio and Pennsylvania, areas that get *very* cold in the winter. The homes are not all crammed together as you see in the city, with no concern at all with alignment to the sun, local wind currents, underground water, and so on. Instead, their homes are built to take advantage of the natural sunlight, so large south-facing windows and workshops are common. Houses are built with entryways, vestibules, and service porches, all those pre-entry spaces that also serve as buffers to keep the cold out and the heat in.

Modern Amish houses are built with 2 by 6 studs and very thick insulation to retain heat. In Peter's area, the windows are double-pane and vinyl. House siding is also vinyl and has insulation under it; caulking is very tight as well. They build their houses tight, and then they seal off windows and doors to keep in the heat. They use double fabric on the windows—a white curtain pulled back to one side and a dark curtain (green,

A SOLAR SPACE HEATER

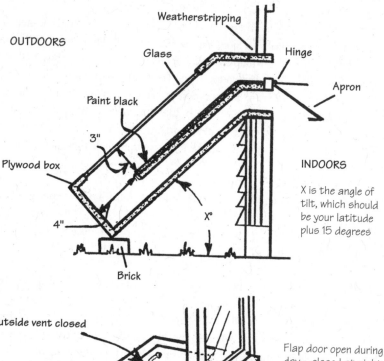

Weatherstripping

OUTDOORS

Glass

Hinge

Apron

Paint black

3"

Plywood box

INDOORS

X is the angle of tilt, which should be your latitude plus 15 degrees

4"

X°

Brick

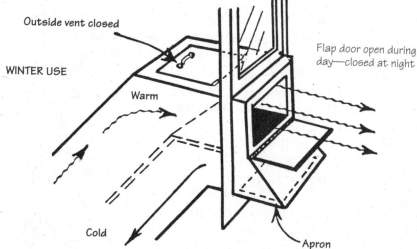

Outside vent closed

Flap door open during day—closed at night

WINTER USE

Warm

Cold

Apron

This box is placed outside of a south-facing window to direct solar-heated air inside. This system can also be used for summer cooling; by opening the outside vent and closing the inside flap door, warmer inside air flows outward.

blue, brown, sometimes light blue) that they pull down to retain heat or coolness, depending on the season. Again, house design is perhaps the single most important factor in creating a home environment that is comfortable in both winter and summer.

Amish homes are heated with space heaters/furnaces that use wood or coal. Cooking during the spring, summer, and early fall is done with Coleman camp stoves and kerosene kitchen stoves, but many families have a woodstove that they use in the winter. The older children, both boys and girls, split the wood for the stove. They go out to the woodpile and refill the wood box each day.

Fires are banked at night before going to bed, which keeps the house warm until morning. Once the fire is going well, extra logs are added and packed tight, and the damper and draft vents are closed, cutting back oxygen and slowing down the burn rate.

"When I first started visiting with the Amish in the evening," says Peter, "the temperature in the house was around 80 degrees F. When I left around 10 P.M., it was still around the same temperature. After a while, I was invited to stay overnight and discovered that the coals were still active enough to ignite new logs at 6 A.M., and the temperature was somewhere in the mid 60s to 70 degrees, even on very cold mornings.

"Many Amish are now using small solar panels to recharge their batteries (for the buggy, power tools, and so on), and some have set up small businesses in which they recharge other people's batteries to help recoup some of the costs of their solar systems."

Although many people are "talking green" today, this is a result of how little action was taken in regards to the environment over the past forty years. We knew about increasing population and dwindling resources back then, and there were many proclamations and alarming statements about the consequences. All the talk, however, did very little to alter our basic way of building our homes, businesses, cars, and communities. We spoke about change but continued in the status quo. Fortunately, this is finally changing, not by government decree, but by ordinary individuals like you and me—pioneers of the quiet revolution—who are choosing to embrace a sustainable lifestyle.

3

BEGINNING FROM
THE BEGINNING

When camping out in the woods, with no electricity or plumbing, I have learned how little we actually *need*. I have always wanted to bring this insight back home, and I've found that it's actually enjoyable and challenging to learn how well I can live with less and less. I lived on my grandfather's farm in somewhat primitive conditions and subsequently realized that I was more aware of the world around me when I was not surrounded by modern appliances. I lived in a house in the hills of Los Angeles for a year and a half as a "squatter," producing much of my own food, recycling everything, keeping the bills ridiculously low by having only essential appliances, and even using a nonflush toilet.

As I experimented in these situations, I became acutely aware that most people on the planet live their daily lives with no air-conditioning, no central heating, no refrigerator, and none of the other things that average middle-class Americans consider so essential. Far from feeling deprived when I used less and less, I found that I was getting more out of my resources, and by extension, I was gaining practical insight out of every experience. I was living more economically, realizing I would not have to adjust much if "the world came to an end," and simply feeling good because my actions were karma-positive—I was one small part of the solution.

I was, and still am, very interested in getting more out of less for several fundamental reasons. First is the survival perspective. What do I really need for basic survival? Must I really have a houseful of expensive material possessions in order to live well? I discovered that when I did not focus on *things*, I was free to explore learning, developing my skills, and interacting with people. I also found that my pursuit of whatever I thought was important in life was costing me less!

Today, we are learning from many sources that the vast numbers of people on this planet, all mostly pursuing more and more *things*, is a significant factor in making our earth increasingly more unlivable. As revealed in Al Gore's documentary, *An Inconvenient Truth*, overpopulation and overconsumption are leading us down the path of destruction. The "green" talk so prevalent today is all based on what we knew decades ago but is now finally starting to get people's attention.

If our addiction to stuff is part of the problem, how do we pursue the solution? If you want to live your life as a solution to our many problems, where do you begin?

Before you start planning an alternate system for your household, you should seriously examine your current electrical usage. You should find ways to reduce your electrical use and make sure that every appliance you have is energy efficient. Otherwise, you will be trying to build a system that far exceeds your actual needs.

As actor and environmentalist Ed Begley, Jr. says, just start from the beginning. Do one thing at a time. Don't expect to get it all handled yesterday. First you must examine how you currently use resources and find the most efficient way to use what you currently have.

In this chapter, we'll address our use of electricity and electrical appliances. In many cases, you'll find that you can live better on less. We're going to attempt to discern what you want from what you actually need. You might be surprised to learn that you don't actually need to consume as much electricity as you think. You can reduce your electrical consumption by a combination of wise use, non-use, conservation, and by increasing your awareness of natural principles.

OUR LOVE OF ELECTRICAL GADGETS

If you already live in some remote cabin and you don't have electricity or electrical appliances, then you don't need this book. You've already figured out that life will go on without electricity. You've learned that you can simply do without or that most of your needs can be handled with hand-operated tools.

If this is not the case, however, you will need to change your perceptions about what you require to live a satisfied—yet also an ecological and economical—life. You want to be more self-reliant, but it all seems so complex, confusing, and expensive. So let's start with our use of electrical appliances. If we select these appliances carefully and reject others, we can improve the quality of our lives while still making a positive contribution to the health of the environment.

Three Considerations

1. *Forgo some electrical devices.* This may mean you need to slightly alter your behavior and take the time to consider if a nonelectric device or appliance will work just as well, if not better, than the electric one you use.

2. *Use your existing appliances more efficiently.* This, too, may require some changes in your habits, but once you realize the cost of your inefficiency and waste, you'll not only feel good it, you'll also be saving money.

3. *Buy the most energy-efficient appliances you can find.* This step will involve a higher initial outlay of cash, but it will save you money and energy over time.

Lights

We've all heard this suggestion before—from Al Gore to the principal at the local elementary school—you will save energy by switching every lightbulb in your house from incandescents to fluorescents.

At the local hardware store or supermarket, you will generally pay about four to five times more to purchase a fluorescent bulb than an incandescent one. Some people will just react to the higher price, say "Whoa!" and then reach for the incandescents.

But let's try to think about the long-term benefits instead of just the immediate out-of-pocket expense. A fluorescent bulb will last about five times as long as an incandescent, and they use about one-quarter the power. Modern fluorescents are as bright as comparable incandescents, but they do not give off the same kind of heat.

When I had all incandescents in my home, it seemed that I was constantly changing the burned-out bulbs. An incandescent bulb never lasted

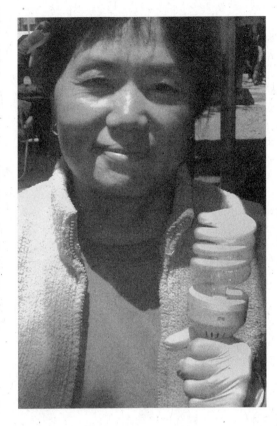

Vang Xiong holds a compact fluorescent bulb.

more than nine months or so, if that. Since then, I have been using some of the same compact fluorescent bulbs in my home for over four years now. These provide sufficient light and don't break as easily as the incandescents.

Once you start to produce your own power, you'll find that you'll automatically think about every use of energy. You'll end up wanting to conserve electricity whenever possible. Switching all your incandescent bulbs to fluorescents is an easy first step.

A large part of energy self-reliance has to do with self-control and discipline. This needn't be painful, but it does require exerting the mental discipline to get yourself accustomed to a new habit. For example, turn the lights off when you won't be returning to a room.

Nonstandard Lighting

Electricity is not the only way to light your home. Part of the problem we face today is overspecialization and lack of interdisciplinary thinking in regards to building homes. Have you ever been in an Amish home or workspace? Since they choose to use no electricity, they build their homes to take advantage of as much natural lighting as possible. Although this may not be possible in all settings, it is obviously an under-utilized method of bringing light inside. Simply designing our houses to face the sun—typically south—and having large south-facing windows allow us to get the maximum amount of light indoors by virtue of the design alone.

There are also the traditional standbys that most people think of only in emergencies: candles and lanterns. Tim Matson wrote an excellent book called *The Book of Non-Electric Lighting: The Classic Guide to the Safe Use of Candles, Fuel Lamps, Lanterns, Gas Lights, and Fireview Stoves, Second Edition* (Countryman, 2008). He describes the various kerosene and paraffin wax lamps, as well as the unique Aladdin lamp. Aladdin lamps are perhaps the only light source you'll find comparable to an incandescent bulb. It's the same lamp that revolutionized oil lighting more than a century ago and is still the lamp of choice for many backwoods residents.

For those of you who are not ready to shell out the money for an Aladdin lamp, you can purchase an ordinary oil lamp at just about any hardware store. These are inexpensive, can be operated with a variety of oils, and should last a lifetime if you take care of them.

Slush lamps—containers for liquid oil into which you insert a wick and light it—are also simple to make.

Matson also includes information on how to make your own candles. Candles are easy to make, either by dipping or using molds. Dipping your wick into the wax, layer by layer, produces a better and more efficient candle than using a mold would. If you choose to make molded candles, however, you can use just about anything as a mold: frozen juice containers, margarine tubs, toilet paper rolls, and so on. Whole books have been written about candle-making, though you really don't need a book to be able to make candles. Early pioneers made candles using rendered animal lard.

Of course, the problem with these forms of lighting is that you could bump them, causing them to tip over and start a fire. You should always exercise extreme caution whenever you are using open flames for lighting. In my opinion, firelight is ideal for camping or for emergencies when at home. But there are far better and safer ways to light our homes that don't pose the same danger as fire.

Light Tubes

Light tubes are installed from the roof to the ceiling of a room. During the day, they bring the light into the kitchen or living room so you don't need to use electricity. This is a relatively simple way to bring light inside when it's light outside.

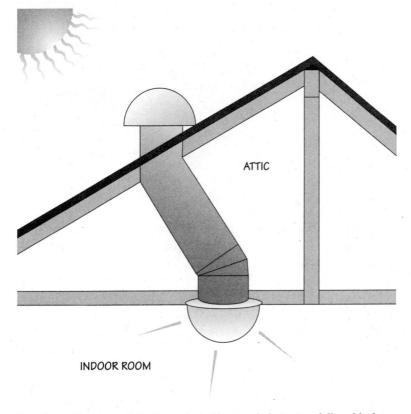

The dome directs sunlight through the ductwork, bringing diffused light into the room.

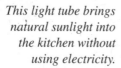

This light tube brings natural sunlight into the kitchen without using electricity.

Solatube is one source for a light tube. The following is their description of how it works: "The Solatube Daylighting System captures sunlight on the rooftop and redirects it down a reflective tube into interior spaces. The tubing will fit between rafters and install easily with no structural modification. At the ceiling level, an attractive diffuser spreads the light evenly throughout the room."

I experienced the wonder of light tubes in two of the homes I visited for this book. In Julia Russell's Eco-Home in Los Angeles, the light tube softly lights the kitchen, bringing natural light indoors during the daytime. It provided sufficient light for any kitchen work.

In Ted Baumgart's home in La Crescenta, I attempted to turn off the light when I departed his bathroom and wondered why the light stayed on. His bathroom was brightly lit from the sunlight coming in through the light tube. I was once again amazed that so many "experts" say such simple technologies are impractical.

In most cases, handy homeowners can install a light tube in a few hours. The tubing can be as long as 30 feet from the roof to the room ceiling, and there are several sizes available. Of course, the brightness of the light inside will vary depending on the brightness of the sun at any moment and on the length of the tubing.

Amish Lighting

During my tour of Amish lands with Peter Gail in 1999, where we visited some of the woodshops and stores in rural Ohio (Amish eschew electricity and instead use lanterns for light; most of their work tools are hand-operated), I was most impressed by the manner in which they built their homes and workspaces. Large windows were on the south sides of the workspaces, facing the sun and taking advantage of natural light as much as possible. How many of today's architects and developers ever take a building's orientation to sunlight into consideration?

Refrigerators

By some accounts, refrigerators are the most inefficient appliances in modern households, although many newer models have improved upon the basic design.

For example, manufacturers tend to build a refrigerator to fit into a specific spot in the modern kitchen. In order to give the refrigerator the most inside space, they tend to make the walls of the refrigerator thinner than would be ideal. A thicker-walled refrigerator holds the cold better (similar to a thick icebox used for camping). Less insulation means you're using more electricity to keep the food cool.

Another problem is that cold descends, so the very nature of the vertical door is inefficient. Most people, however, won't buy an icebox-style refrigerator with a lid on the top for their kitchens. This also leads to the question of why the frozen section of the refrigerator is usually at the top. It is usually there out of tradition, but it is a poor design. Some refrigerators are designed with the freezer section at the bottom, which makes more sense.

Refrigerators create cold by repelling heat off the coils that are usually found on the back of the refrigerators. When you purchase a refrigerator, find out if you need to periodically dust off the back coils (on some, this is not necessary). If you let dust accumulate, you are insulating the coils and thereby making your refrigerator work harder to keep the food cold. If you need to periodically dust off the coils, make sure you have wheels on the bottom of the refrigerator so you can easily pull it out from the wall to clean.

If you are buying a new refrigerator, look for the Energy Star rating and buy the most efficient one you can afford. Yes, you may initially spend a little more for an efficient model, but you will be paying less on your electrical bill month after month after month.

Our friend Chanel Patricia purchased an old house in the hilly section of Highland Park overlooking the Arroyo Seco. She had some very specific ideas when she remodeled her home; she wanted the design to help facilitate her desire for self-reliance. She discovered that the old house had a traditional vegetable cooler, which appears to be an ordinary built-in kitchen cabinet. When you opened the door, however, the shelves were made of wire mesh, and there was one vent that opened into the basement and another that opened into the attic. This allowed a natural airflow where the cooler air from the basement rises and flows to the attic. This was an old-fashioned, low-tech way to keep foods cool that didn't absolutely need refrigeration—a method all but forgotten by modern builders.

Chanel also chose to have no refrigerator at all. At first, I was surprised to hear this because at the time I stored so many frozen foods. But Chanel told me that she was concerned when her research showed that the refrigerator was the biggest energy consumer in the home. She was determined to create a home and a lifestyle that was energy-efficient, so she opted for no refrigerator. She did this by utilizing just about all the time-tested means of food preservation.

She purchased lots of dried foods, usually in bulk so she wouldn't have to run to the store every day. Her cupboards were full of rice, noodles, soups, crackers, dried fruits and nuts, and so on. Just about any food today can be purchased in cans, so she stocked up on these as well. This included milk, soup, pasta sauces, olives, fruit preserves, and vegetables.

Chanel did purchase perishable foods in small amounts from a local market that was about one city block away, a walk of approximately five minutes. She would store them in her vegetable cooler and use them within forty-eight hours of purchase. This included such items as fresh vegetables, fruit, salad greens, milk, cheese, and kefir.

Once when Dolores and I visited Chanel, we noticed that she had perishable items in a dishpan partly filled with water and covered with a wet towel. This was her simple form of an evaporative cooler, which was an effective way to keep such things as butter, cheese, and other dairy products cool.

We always admired what she did all by herself, constantly finding ways to recycle, save energy, and explore how to do more with less. (Chanel passed away from cancer in 1996—we still miss her.)

Other Kitchen Appliances

Electric Can Openers. Ever hear of someone who couldn't even open some canned goods after a power outage because all he or she had was an electric can opener? Buy a good manual can opener and keep it handy. Most Swiss Army knives also have a blade specifically designed for opening cans—and everyone has a Swiss Army knife, don't they?

Electric knife sharpeners. For the most part, these cause damage to quality knives. Get rid of them!

Electric juicers. I'll admit that some of these are quite good, such as the Acme and Vitamix juicers. You simply couldn't achieve the same result manually. Still, if you simply want to make orange juice or grapefruit juice from the fresh fruit, buy the simple devices wherein you cut the fruit in half and twist it around the cone to extract the juice.

Microwave ovens. There is still some controversy about using microwave ovens to cook food. It is also worth noting that microwaves are generally suited to cooking highly processed "fast foods," which are more expensive and less nutritious than whole foods. Part of becoming energy self-reliant is to rethink everything we do, how we do it, and why we do it. Since good food, properly prepared, is so fundamental to good health and well-being, shouldn't we examine why we are so rushed that we feel compelled to use microwave ovens?

While most people consider growing food an essential part of self-reliance, they don't seem to understand that we have lost the idea about the sacredness of food. The alchemy that takes place in the kitchen when we transform these products into something else entirely should not only

Every household should have plenty of hand tools, such as the can opener, juicer, and grater shown here.

sustain our bodies, but also our souls. This alchemical transformation—from food for the body to food for the soul—is nearly impossible to achieve with a microwave. Our choice to embrace this fast-food culture is one of our many choices that has diminished our sense of self-reliance.

Automatic dishwashers. There are some dishwashers that are energy-efficient, and if you insist on having one, you should get the most energy-efficient model possible. I have found that it is somewhat meditative to stand before the sink where I can look out the window, silently wash each dish, rinse it, and let it drip-dry in the dish rack. I then carry the dish pan outside and pour the used water on the plants in the yard (we choose detergents that are safe for the soil). Doing all this by hand doesn't take a particularly long time, and it keeps me in touch with the elements of my own life.

Using an automatic dishwasher may seem to free us to do other things, but what is life really all about? This is something we each need to answer for ourselves, in our own private lives. But once we find ourselves enslaved to an appliance that we believe we "can't live without," it's probably time to consider practical alternatives.

Stoves. With gas stoves, use the smallest flame possible and always keep all pots and pans covered while you cook. This not only saves gas, but also reduces scorching the pots and pans. I recall a sign in a kitchen that said "If you can smell it, you're losing it." This was an admonishment to keep all cooking foods covered, because if the aromas were in the air, they were no longer in the food.

Garbage disposals. These are fuel hogs that also use up lots of water, simply so your compost can get washed away. You should add all your kitchen scraps to your compost pit or worm farm. I have long believed that the main function of garbage disposals is to keep plumbers employed. In the homes I have owned, I always removed the garbage disposals, put the

Julia Russell shows visitors her garden and large composters at her Eco-Home.

A commercial composter used in the author's yard.

Another type of commercial composter.

kitchen scraps in the compost pit (or fed them to the chickens), and had fewer plumbing problems as a result.

Having a compost pit or worm farm in the backyard is one of the easiest ways to be part of the ecological solution. Every residential backyard in America should have one. They are easy to make, use, and maintain. It isn't necessary to buy a commercial composter since a simple compost system is easy to make.

In an elevated society of the future, I envision a composter as the norm for every backyard. It is the ancient way in which each plot of land can be enriched by the alchemical conversion of the residents' wastes. In the interrelated network of permaculture, we should continue to find multiple uses for the resources we use each day. Much of our household wastewater should water our gardens, and we should be able to produce most of the fertilizer we need by composting our kitchen scraps. When Dolores and I moved into our new home in 1987, one of the first things we did was construct our large compost pit/worm farm.

Washers and Dryers

When purchasing a new washing machine, look for the best Energy Star rating. Some of the newer models are more efficient with both electricity and water.

If you are able to do so in your location, you should disconnect your washing machine drain from the sewer line and direct the rinse water into your yard to water your garden. This is easy to do and allows you to reuse the water used to wash your clothes.

If you choose to transfer the rinse water to your yard, here are a few things to keep in mind:

1. Buy a detergent that is not toxic to plants in your yard.
2. Don't allow water to puddle up somewhere and breed mosquitoes.
3. Test your system to make sure it works and drains well and doesn't overstrain the washing machine.

Rich Redman shows off his LG Electronics front-loading washing machine. It has an Energy Star rating and uses less water than an average washing machine. It has no belts and is powered instead by gears. Redman directs all of the used wash water into his yard.

Julia Russell with her "solar clothes dryer."

You can generally attach a large hose to the drain line of the washing machine; this new hose should be at least as large in diameter as your washing machine's drain hose. It must also be long enough for gravity to get it to your yard.

Remember, everything is related to everything else. In the *Extreme Simplicity* book I wrote with Dolores, I discuss how taking baths is more healthful than showers and how I always wash a few garments by hand every time I take a bath. I do this automatically, using water that has already been heated. This means that I get more than one use from my bath water. (Sometimes I even use that water a third time to flush the toilet.) It also means that I don't have to use my washing machine as often.

When purchasing a clothes dryer, look for the best Energy Star rating available. But don't overlook the utter practicality of the "solar clothes dryer"—a clothesline!

During a winter visit to the Ohio Amish lands, I was very impressed to see that every Amish household dries their clothes on their covered porches, on racks specifically devised for this purpose. They have committed themselves to not using electricity, so they find those natural forces and natural principles, which they then use for their day-to-day needs. No gas or electricity is needed to dry their garments, and they get the benefit of the sun's UV rays to sterilize their clothes.

Garage and Yard Tools

Many of today's garage tools are powered by built-in batteries that can be recharged over and over. Some can even be set up to be recharged by the sun. This includes such tools as drills, saws, pneumatic hammers, staplers, and more. With a small photovoltaic system, you can keep all your tools powered by the sun.

I have a very dim view of such "garden tools" as weed whackers and leaf blowers. Though such tools have a place, too often I have seen weed whackers used around trees, which damages the cambium layer around the base of the tree and occasionally kills it. To me, traditional methods of

Jeff Booth uses a rake, not a leaf blower.

pruning and pulling weeds seem better than weed whackers. As for leaf blowers, among the noise, dust, fumes, and the number of times I have watched a "gardener" simply blow leaves and dirt into the street or into a neighbor's yard, I see no need for these contraptions. I am not a proponent of blowers and don't feel we'd be culturally deprived if they all disappeared.

I prefer hand tools for pruning and a rake and broom for cleaning. When called upon to cut the lawn, I have used both push mowers and power mowers, though my belief about the pointlessness of "front lawns" keeps me from endorsing such devices.

Other Electronics

Most electronics in modern homes are not energy hogs. Still, you should do your research before making purchases. By buying the most energy-efficient products, you will save money on your power bills. And by buy-

An ornate style of an independent (not wired) solar lamp for an outdoor walkway.

ing the best quality you can afford, your products will last many years, and you will not be contributing (as much) to the landfill.

Solar Gadgets

Today you can purchase a vast array of stand-alone products that are independently powered by the sun. These include lights for walkways, entryways, small ceiling fans, radios, flashlights, trickle-chargers for your car's battery, chargers for your cell phone, and more. Such photovoltaic-powered products can usually be found at your local hardware store.

Some of these—like a trickle battery charger—should be a standard part of every automobile. Others—like a solar charger for your cell phone—are essential for communications during a blackout or in the aftermath of an earthquake. During a recent blackout in my area, my cell phone needed to be charged. I was able to make calls by sitting on my front porch with my cell phone plugged into a solar panel.

A wonderful Freeplay radio that can be powered either by the sun (see top panel), by cranking, or by batteries.

Al Strange shows a solar panel that connects to a car's cigarette lighter socket. It provides a trickle-charge to the battery. This is especially important if the car will be sitting unused for long periods of time.

Jeff Philipp talks on a cell phone connected to a car recharger, which in turn is connected to a small solar panel.

Cell phone connected to a car jack (designed to plug into a cigarette lighter socket), which is connected to a small solar panel.

OFF THE GRID

A lot can be done to improve your home's energy efficiency before you even think about installing solar panels. Your first step is to conduct an energy survey of your home. Your energy survey shows you how much energy you are currently using and thereby gives you a good idea of how to design your alternative electrical system. Remember that if you can reduce your energy usage and use more efficient appliances, you will not have to build as large a system.

According to Glenn Forbes, one way to determine how to size your system is to start with your power bill. It will tell you your daily consumption; for example, you might average 15 to 30 kilowatts per day.

Joel Davidson and Richard Komp, authors of *The Solar Electric Home: A Photovoltaics How-to Handbook*, provide a simple way to size a system:

1. Determine your loads or power requirements.
2. Based on your requirements, decide how large of a PV array is needed.
3. Size your battery storage.

In order to further quantify the power requirements in number one, they suggest the following:

1. List the devices you wish to power.
2. List the power requirements of each device.
3. List the number of hours you intend to use each item.

This analysis is the essence of the power survey. A simple version is presented here for your use.

POWER SURVEY

AC Electrical device	Device watts	×	Hours of daily use	×	Days of use per week	Divided by 7	=	Average watt-hours per day
		×		×			=	
		×		×			=	
		×		×			=	
		×		×			=	
		×		×			=	
		×		×			=	
		×		×			=	
		×		×			=	
		×		×			=	
		×		×			=	
		×		×			=	
		×		×			=	

You simply add rows until you've recorded every appliance you expect to power. And don't forget about "ghost loads"—those appliances that are on all the time, such as clocks, televisions, automatic coffee makers, and so on. Anything with a clock or timer is on all the time, even if it's not being actively used. Add up all the figures in the far right column. That total will be used to determine the required size of your system. Another option would be to do your research and then buy as much as you can afford.

4

ALTERNATIVES TO GRID ELECTRICITY

Now that you've completed your home energy survey, you should have a good idea of your household's energy use. Before you begin your plans to build an alternative electrical system, you still have a few decisions to make, such as whether you're going to produce electricity from the sun, the wind, or pedal power.

THE SUN

Solar electricity is produced from the free electrons of specially made silicon wafers or chips, which can then be tapped for our electrical needs. The silicon wafers are typically installed in panels or modules that are measured by the expected wattage. Several of these modules are wired together to make an array, and there are no moving parts. Maintenance is minimal and includes such things as simply keeping dust off the surface of the module.

Two reasons that photovoltaic (PV) electricity is not more widely used today are the initial cost and the assumptions regarding the impracticality of solar energy. The cost for PV has steadily dropped; the cost to produce a watt in the year 2000, for example, was one-tenth of what it cost in 1955. According to many calculations, it's still more expensive than using fossil fuels for power, though not everyone analyzes *all* the costs of conventional versus solar electricity. Some analysts say that there will be no great reduction in cost or great rise in solar-panel efficiency in the near future, but a PV system is still useful if you plan it carefully.

THE WIND

Brian Hurd, who teaches a photovoltaic installer certification program at the East Los Angeles Skills Center, says that although wind is a viable way to create electricity, no one wants to live where wind is readily available. "If it's a viable place for wind electricity," he says, "you probably can't hear your own voice in a conversation." Although this is an exaggeration, PV systems are far simpler and more abundant than wind machines.

By wind machines, I do not mean the massive towers power companies use in the desert but instead the sort of apparatus one can put on top of a garage to produce electricity. There are off-the-shelf models out there as well as many do-it-yourself plans that have been around for decades.

The do-it-yourself plans involve attaching an alternator to a tower—you do not want to attach a wind machine directly to your roof or any part of your home because of its sound and vibrations. Propeller-style blades spin the alternator when the wind is blowing. The size of the batteries determines how much potential power your system can produce; you can typically produce 12, 24, or 48 volts of direct current (VDC) in such an arrangement. You are essentially charging the batteries, then using the energy produced. You would also need an inverter and over-current protection devices (OCPDs) to power an average household.

Proponents of wind energy state that wind machines will outlast PV systems, but PV supporters point out that there is hardly any maintenance required with PV. Wind devices have to be shut down in high winds, must be lubricated and painted occasionally, and do not work if there is no wind. Wind systems might therefore not be right for every household, but they are certainly viable if the right system is located in the right place. Rural areas seem to be the best locations for wind power. More information on wind-powered energy can be found at www.windstreampower.com.

PEDAL POWER

I spoke with Dave Strom of Norwalk, California, who has built several pedal-power systems for generating electricity. Dave offered an explanation of how pedal power developed and what its future might be.

In times of emergency or high power costs, the idea of generating power by pedaling a bicycle returns. Today, the idea of "green" power is growing and can take some of the pressure off the existing grid. Dave has built a number of bike generators as well as other small emergency power systems. Let's take a look at the uses and practicality of bike-powered generators.

History

"People-powered" tools have been in use for more than a century. Most people have seen treadle sewing machines, many of which are still in use. Bike power has been used for scroll saws as well as washing machines. Almost anything that needed a small motor has been powered by a bike at one time.

During World War II and after, hand-crank generators were used to power radios. At times, soldiers repositioned the generator so they could pedal it with their feet. However, this was neither common nor practical as the operator would have to widely spread his feet on either side of the generator, making pedaling difficult.

During the Cold War in the 1950s and '60s, use of a bike to charge batteries and provide ventilation became commonplace. This was, and still is, a practical solution for fallout shelters. At that time, solar panels were not available to the public, and bike power was the only available option. Some government shelters were equipped with tandem bikes set up with ventilation fans.

Throughout the 1960s, alternative power sources were explored extensively. Many bike generators were cobbled together using generators or alternators from cars. Magazines such as the original *Mother Earth News* carried articles on these projects. Throughout the following decades, these ideas have resurfaced many times. Suppliers come and go—most disappear never to be seen again.

Today

Fuel costs have skyrocketed and the power grids are strained to failure. Our population has grown tremendously, yet emergency services have not expanded enough to cover these needs. Such agencies are now overwhelmed on a daily basis. The bottom line is that the average American is going to be on his or her own in an emergency, possibly for a long time. A bike generator may fit into some people's emergency response strategy well.

A Simple Electrical Theory

The other use for a bike generator is "green" power. Any power provided by alternative means takes some load off the existing sources. Electrical power comes in two usable forms for the average person. The first is 110 volts alternating current (110 VAC). This is what you use at home to plug in your television or toaster. The second is direct current (DC) such as you have available in your car or from a battery. This is typically 12 volts (12 VDC) in a car or truck. There are a few exceptions, such as old Volkswagens (6 VDC) and some military vehicles (24 VDC).

Alternating current can travel over great distances without too much loss, but it can't be stored—it must be used as it is generated. Direct current cannot travel very far but can be stored in batteries.

A DC motor usually becomes a generator if the armature is turned. This is done via the shaft sticking out from the center. Dayton DC motors were used in bike generators years ago. Modifying an old cordless drill motor might be a way to recycle these tools. Other cordless tools should work as well.

The output from any DC motor will likely be close to the power required to run that motor. So if you have a cordless tool that uses a 7.2-volt battery, it will likely produce the same amount if the motor is turned by a bike or other source. There will likely be a blocking diode or other electronics in the tool to prevent such use, so you will need to remove these parts. There are too many tools on the market to make any specific recommendations.

Available or Do-It-Yourself Systems

Most systems, whether you build it or buy it, typically take one of two forms. The first is a stationary bike and the second is a stand in which you mount your existing bike. In either case, there is a generator usually mounted on a "swing arm." The arm simply pivots down to the tire, and its own weight holds it down on the tire as you pedal.

The size of the generator varies from different dealers. You need to calculate the output from your set and decide how long you need to pedal to generate your energy needs—or at least what you can provide with the time available. There is no standard on these sets to quote, so you'll need to "do the math" with Ohm's law to determine your needs and capabilities.

The bike generator sets made in the past were very generic and would fit most bikes, but they required twenty minutes to set up and break down. There are bike stands available today that allow you to convert your road bike to a stationary exercise bike. This is done very quickly but will only work on bikes with quick release hubs.

Your battery system is beyond the scope of this section, but for a small system a bike could help keep batteries charged. The pedaling time needed to fully charge batteries could be considerable. If you have one of the small portable power packs with a battery rated at 10 AH and a bike generator with an output of 1 AH, for example, you'd need to pedal all day to charge it! This is very unlikely in the real world and in an emergency there's really too many other things to focus on.

The Real World

If you have a fallout-type shelter, a bike generator and/or ventilation system is a great idea. People will need the exercise and all the power that can be created. If you use regular bikes for this, they will be needed after it's safe to exit the shelter. If you use an exercise bike or stationary stand now, adding a generator and charging a small power pack is viable. You have taken some strain off the grid and you would be using the bike anyway. This "time factor" is the key to practical use.

There are currently companies advertising a bike generator setup with a laptop computer in use. Another ad shows a receptionist in an office building pedaling away while answering the phone and scheduling meetings on a PC. Yet another ad shows a small television connected to the bike with a caption telling you to have the kids pedal if they want to watch TV.

While these all seem like great ideas, I can't imagine they're at all practical. The ergonomics simply don't work out. How is an employer to get all this to work out with employees? Power is used to multitask. Your washing machine at home does the work while you do other things. If you had to pedal a bike to make the power to wash the clothes, you may as well be using a washboard.

Going Forward

As a practical matter, a bike generator only works if you are riding anyway. So if you use a stationary bike now, adding a generator should work out well. But if you ride a regular bike, you don't have that option. This is currently an untapped area—if a small generator were set up on a bike, you could charge batteries while on the road.

The problem with doing this is in the weight of the rig, including the battery and mounting hardware. In addition, the generator would likely be bouncing about while on the road. But on fairly smooth pavement it could work well. As mentioned earlier, a DC motor from a cordless tool might be modified to be used as a small DC generator on a road bike. A 7.2 VDC motor might work well to charge Ham radio handheld batteries, which are also 7.2 VDC.

A small battery—12 VDC at about 7 AH in size—would be light enough to strap to a rear cargo rack. Battery holders can be cobbled together to hold whatever you might need.

The old friction generator for bike headlights might be modified for charging a couple of NiCad or similar batteries. These are still available, and many turn up at yard sales.

All batteries also need some way to control the charge. You will likely use some existing charging circuit or equipment and modify it to suit your needs.

In Closing

Bike generators can be practical in the right situation. During extended emergencies, cordless tools will be idle and can be converted to develop some power for radios and other small electronics. Anything done today to relieve the strain from the power grid is good, and recycling tools or other damaged equipment reduces landfill waste.

CHOOSING THE RIGHT SYSTEM

Deciding which method of home-energy production will work best for you depends on several factors, such as the length of time the wind blows each day in your area, the amount of sunlight you get on your roof each day, your skills, your budget, and so on. You then need to decide whether you are going to build a stand-alone system, your own power station, or a grid-connected system, the latter of which allows you to share collected energy with your energy provider.

Stand-Alone Systems

If you plan to use a PV system to generate electricity, you will need solar modules and a mounting system suitable for your roof type or yard space. You will also need batteries, a charge controller, an inverter, wires, connectors, and safety devices. Your solar modules will generate 12 to 48 VDC, which the inverter will convert to 110 or 220 volts of alternating current (VAC), the standard amount of energy for most modern households. The modules charge the batteries during the day, and the inverter then draws power from the batteries when necessary. In a stand-alone system, the batteries and charge controller are the heart of the system.

You could build a stand-alone system that is entirely 12 VDC, but the result would be similar to living in a car or trailer. Nearly all homes are wired for 110 VAC today, so you'd only take the 12-VDC route if you were building a remote home from scratch. Since the majority of appliances are designed for 110 VAC, all of your appliances would have to be made for 12 VDC, such as those designed for recreational vehicles. Such systems are antiquated; you can instead purchase a smaller, less expensive inverter in addition to gas-powered generators for special applications.

Connected to the Grid

Today, as much as 95-plus percent of solar rooftop systems are grid-connected and do not use batteries. This means that the modules generate electricity, but no electrical energy is stored in the batteries for emergencies. The net inverter measures how much electricity your system generates, then compares that amount with how much electricity you actually use. Your electric bill is then determined by how much electricity you use beyond what you produce. In this kind of system, the inverter is the heart of the system. (You should discuss the policy on this matter with the electric company to make sure your bill is an exact amount rather than an estimate.)

In theory, your system should still produce electricity during a blackout. Due to "anti-islanding," however, your grid-connected solar system will also go down in a blackout to protect power company employees from being surprised and electrocuted by your system when the rest of the power in the neighborhood is out.

SYSTEM COMPONENTS

Solar Modules

The photo below shows the "panels" of wired silicon wafers that generate electricity when they are exposed to the sun. In a stand-alone system, 50 percent of the cost will go toward the solar module and 40 percent will go toward the batteries. In a grid-connected system, expect the cost of the modules to be about 70 percent of the total cost.

Christopher Nyerges displays a Solarex solar module.
SUE REDMAN

Solar cells can be either the thin-film type with an efficiency of about 8 percent, or a crystalline cell with an efficiency of about 15 to 20 percent. "Efficiency" refers to the amount of sunlight striking the cell that is actually turned into electricity. Most solar experts advise you not to get too hung up on efficiency, however, except in those cases where you have an extremely limited amount of space in which to place your solar modules. A greater concern is your cost per watt. At the time this book was written, there were a limited number of solar-module manufacturing companies. If you are on a budget, any brand will do. The panels mix and match without problems. When buying new, purchase them by the pallet if possible for better pricing.

Batteries

Stand-alone systems require batteries. These components will make up as much as 40 percent of your total cost depending on your demand for power. The energy from your solar array, your wind device, and even from your pedaling is stored in the battery for later use. When the lights go out, the batteries provide your power.

When you purchase batteries, you do not want car batteries—you want "deep-cycle" batteries. Deep-cycle batteries are designed to deliver a consistent voltage as the battery discharges. A variety of battery choices exist, but rechargeable sealed lead-acid and deep-cycle types are best for solar power production.

Lead-Acid

Lead-acid batteries, in either liquid vented or sealed models, resemble standard car batteries. The liquid vented (also called "flooded") batteries vent hydrogen gas when the battery nears full charge, so they must be periodically inspected and refilled with liquid. Also, because of the explosive and corrosive nature of hydrogen gas, these batteries require tremendous amounts of maintenance and safety precautions.

Sealed batteries, however, require no maintenance, and they are spill-proof. The two types of sealed batteries commonly used in PV systems are the gel cell and the absorbed glass mat (AGM). Gel cell batteries cost more per unit of capacity compared with liquid lead-acid batteries. Glenn

Forbes, who uses sealed AGM batteries, says it's permissible to purchase used batteries if you can find them, but they should be no more than a few years old.

Alkaline

Nickel-cadmium and nickel-iron alkaline batteries are also available. They are generally not used, however, in residential PV systems. They are more expensive and are not as affected by changing temperatures as are other batteries. They are typically used in industrial or commercial applications, new cars, or in areas where extremely cold weather is expected.

Inverters

Your inverter will account for about 25 percent of your system cost if you have an off-the-grid system with batteries, and about 10 percent of your cost if your system is tied into the grid without batteries. Sizing your system will determine the breakdown of the percentages for the different components.

Most inverters made for the United States convert 12, 24, or 48 VDC and produce 120 and 220 VAC at 60 hertz. There are many inverters from which to choose, and your choice will depend upon what you are trying to power.

If you plan to do your own labor, be sure to study *Photovoltaics: Design and Installation Manual* and *The Complete Idiot's Guide to Solar Power for Your Home, 2nd Edition* as well as all pertinent aspects of the NEC handbook, article 690. If you plan to hire an electrician, this will give you a working knowledge of your choices. Expect to pay about $10 per watt for installation. Some utility companies charge differently for "peak" time (those hours when electrical usage is highest) than for "off-peak" time (all other hours).

There are two categories of inverters: grid-tied or non-grid-tied and stand-alones (used for powering a system independent of the utility company). Some inverters may be able to operate in several of these categories, but power companies frown upon them.

The type of wave that the inverter produces can also help determine its cost. The three most common are square waves, modified square waves, and sine waves (the best for solar applications).

Xantrex inverters at Glenn Forbes's family home.

Gary Gonzales with a portable 2,500-watt inverter.

Plug-in side of the inverter.

Square Wave

These inexpensive inverters are appropriate only for small appliances, small resistive heating loads, and incandescent lights. They can actually burn up the motors in some equipment, so they are not used in residential systems.

Modified Square Wave

This style of inverter can handle a wide variety of loads, such as lights, motors, televisions, and stereos. It may, however, have some problems with microwaves, clocks, and other electronic devices. Battery packs for cordless tools should not be charged on modified square wave inverters.

Sine Wave

For grid-tied systems, you *must* use a sine-wave inverter. These inverters are used to operate sensitive electronic hardware that requires a high quality waveform. Sine-wave inverters have many advantages over modified-square-wave inverters.

Rick Ulrich of Buel Solar recommends avoiding any of the cheap inverters available, which are typically inexpensive and have no brand name. "These might be okay when you go camping, but they will not last," he says. "They have cheap components, running typically at 170 volts, with a lowered internal voltage, and they are almost running as a square wave inverter." He suggests brand names such as Xantrex (which has purchased Hart, ProSine, and Trace). "There are others, too," says Ulrich, "but they are very expensive. The better ones have 150 to 180 internal voltage, and the modified sine wave is okay if you are getting a brand name." You should expect (as of this writing) to spend $400 to $500 for an inverter.

According to Glenn Forbes, however, "Any of the name brand equipment available today is good, so you just need to find what goes with your pocketbook. New equipment is preferred because of the warranty and replaceability." Forbes says you should "expect to spend between $1,500 to $3,000 for the inverter, depending on your application and power needs. Charge controller, wiring, connectors, circuit breakers, meters, and so on, will be more."

PROFILES OF THOSE
WHO HAVE TAKEN THE PLUNGE

Profile 1: Solar-Powered Electricity

I have long wanted to utilize the sun to produce electricity. In the case of solar photovoltaic panels, I must admit that I was as ignorant as the general public in thinking that all you needed to do was get some panels and "hook them up" in order to utilize the power of the sun. I have received telephone calls telling me that if I hurry I can get in on a deal to buy panels either on sale or wholesale, but I always declined because I wasn't exactly sure what I'd need to complete the job properly and safely.

Half the people in the world today don't have ready access to electricity, which illustrates that we don't actually *need* electricity to live. With this in mind, consider that if you cut your electrical usage in half, you can build a smaller and less expensive PV system to handle your needs. You must first decide, however, what you're trying to achieve with a solar PV system.

For example, you can create a PV system that is wholly independent from the grid, one that is either DC (direct current, the type of current your solar panel produces) or AC (alternating current, which is what most households use). The last option is the most common because most households are already wired to AC, so you would need an inverter to go from DC to AC.

If you are building a remote cabin, you can wire it for DC at the onset, thereby eliminating the need for an inverter and the subsequent 10 percent transfer loss.

Another option is to install a net meter inverter. This is a more expensive inverter that converts the sun's DC current to AC for your household, but it is also wired into the existing power grid. When your rooftop array of panels is producing more power than you are using, it turns your meter backwards. You are therefore *earning* money by being a net power producer.

Each one of these options has its pros and cons. There is no single perfect system; your choice will depend on your needs, your location, and your budget.

In our situation, we wanted to have a simple back-up solar system in the event of power outages, as well as one that would power Dolores's office. We decided to install our system in 1999, when some of the more dire predictions regarding Y2K had much of the industrialized world coming to a standstill.

After much discussion, we purchased a Portawatts 1,000-watt inverter (runs continuously at 800 watts), two 98-amp batteries (rated for 250 cycles, meaning they will last from six to eight years), two 64-watt Uni-Solar panels (should last twenty to twenty-five years), and all the hardware from Solar Webb, Inc. (www.solarwebb.com).

*Two Deka
98-amp batteries.*

Wade Webb installs a 1,000-watt inverter for a small stand-alone system.

Wiring each solar module.

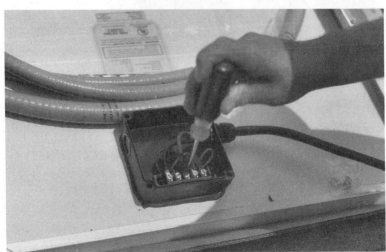

We asked Wade Webb, owner of Solar Webb, to install the system in our northeast Los Angeles home. He first analyzed our roof and determined where to put the two panels, then carefully wired them together. The batteries were connected in parallel, then wired to a controller panel that was mounted on the outside wall near the batteries. Everything was wired into the controller—the batteries, the lines from the panels, and the line leading to the load, which in our case meant the inverter. Webb had to drill a hole through our stucco wall to pass the wires from the controller to the inverter, which was mounted just inside Dolores's office.

We had originally planned to have a system designed to power an office that housed a laptop computer, light, fan, and small cooler. We decided instead, however, to run a Dell Dimension desktop on the system, an incandescent lamp, and the phone machines. We discovered that our PV system would power everything for a few hours before it began to run out of power. We then planned to add a few more panels in order to increase the electricity we were generating and another battery to increase the storage capacity.

Getting the roof prepared for the solar modules.

Securing the modules to the roof.

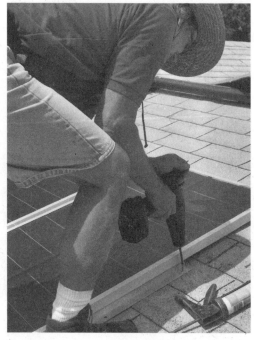

Proper installation is essential.

Webb wires the panels to the control box.

Wiring it all together. Webb is a licensed electrician—be sure you know what you're doing before beginning your project, or hire a professional.

ANALYSIS OF OUR SYSTEM

The production end of the system includes two Uni-Solar 64-watt panels, wired together in a series, equaling a total 128 watts. (The actual CEC rating is 60 watts. This is the difference between the theoretical and the actual wattage you can expect.)

The storage part of the system includes two Deka 12-VDC batteries, rated at 98-amp hours, connected in parallel. Batteries are "derated" at about 20 percent efficiency, which means that you can't take all the power out of them.

One 1,000-watt inverter is used to convert the 12-VDC current to the household power of 110 VAC. The inverter is "derated" between 5 and 10 percent, meaning that only about 800 watts are usable.

One SunSaver 10 Controller, which allows up to 10 amps of PV power into it. Our system's two panels are rated at 3.88 amps; therefore, we will only need to upgrade the controller when we install more panels.

Analysis of Usage

The computer operates at 150 watts per hour. If we run the computer eight hours each day, we use a total of 1,200 watt hours per day.

The two solar panels generate 64 watts each, which equals 128 watts per hour. With approximately five hours of usable sunlight each day, we generate about 640 watt hours.

Therefore, although this system will operate a laptop computer, some lights, a fan, and a telephone machine, it only produces half the power we would need to run the Dell Dimension PC system.

Profile 2: A Grid-Connected Solar Array

Tucked away near the foothills of the Angeles National Forest is the little community of Sierra Madre, California. In the northern part of this community, near the base of mountains, is the home of Renee Cossutta and Debbie Ross. While walking by their home one day, I noticed the array of solar panels on the carport. I boldly went up to the door, knocked, and began to ask questions.

Cossutta had been interested in conservation and localized production for years and had always made the effort to not overuse resources. She'd wanted her own solar electrical system for over a decade. After reading about the adverse effects from the modern ways of generating electricity, she decided she wanted to be a part of the solution.

Some years ago, she contacted the folks at Real Goods in Hopland, California, and asked what it would take to install a solar system. After analyzing the situation, the company determined that it would not be cost-effective to install panels on the roof because there was not enough sunlight there to generate the amount of electricity that would be needed to power the household.

Later, in 2005, Cossutta and Ross realized that an area they had been using for parking received more sun. They once again consulted with the folks at Real Goods and concluded that they *could* create a solar-powered system that would work. An architect friend of theirs designed a combination carport and grape arbor that would support the solar modules. Once the structure was built, the folks from Real Goods installed the solar system. "This was my first opportunity to do something like this," says Cossutta. "It took two days for Real Goods to install our system, and we were very impressed with them."

The system chosen for their household was grid-connected, meaning that no batteries were required. There are fourteen Sharp modules, each rated at 160 watts. The Xantrex inverter, measuring about 18 inches by 3 feet, is connected to the net meter, which is also called a "time of use" meter. During the day, the system feeds electricity into the grid when the two are away at work. Their monthly electric bill shows how much power their system generates and how much electricity they use. Because their power company places a higher value on peak-hour electricity from 10 A.M. to 5 P.M., the women actually get paid more for each peak hour of their generated electricity than what they pay for their off-peak electrical usage.

The entire system, including installation, cost about $12,000. At the time of this writing, it had not yet paid for itself. This will happen when the system is about ten years old, depending on the cost of electricity. It may pay for itself sooner if the price of electricity continues to rise. The two women also received tax credits and rebates from the power company.

Did having a solar electrical system change the way they did things? "Well, we produce our own electricity, and you'd think that we'd no longer worry or think about it. But it has been just the opposite of what I expected. We actually are more careful with our electrical usage now. It's like if you grow your own strawberries in the yard. Yes, you have food, and that's good, but you have to watch them to make sure they grow," says Cossutta. She adds that there is just about no maintenance required for the system, except that occasionally during the dry season, she hoses off accumulated dust. Otherwise, there is nothing else that needs to be done.

She offers the following advice for those who want to pursue solar energy for their own households: "Look online and read about solar

Cossutta with their Xantrex inverter.

Ross (left) and Cossutta with solar array in background.

Ross and Cossutta stand under the carport that supports their solar array.

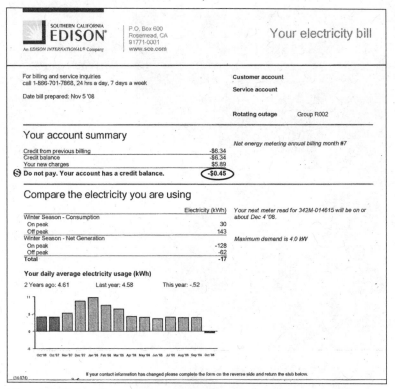

Electric bill showing a credit balance due to Ross and Cossutta. Their small PV system enables them to produce much of their own energy.

electricity. Find out what it means to have solar power. Learn how it pays for itself. Do plenty of research first so you know what you're getting into. Ten years ago, it wasn't so easy to find this information, but today there is a lot of information out there. Go and talk to anyone you know who has done this. And look at the Real Goods catalog, and check them out online."

Profile 3: Solar-Powered Refrigerator

Ted Baumgart lives with his family in La Cresenta, California, a wooded residential area nestled near the foothills of the Angeles National Forest. In 1980, when he analyzed the largest power consumer in the average household, he found that the refrigerator uses twice the energy of any other appliance. The refrigerators that were manufactured in 1980, moreover, were very inefficient.

"I realized that the refrigerator was the power hog, so I read everything I could to find an alternative," says Baumgart. "I read *Mother Earth News*, *Farm News*, and anything I could get my hands on. Then I learned about Larry Schlussler in Arcata, California, who was manufacturing refrigerators that were five times more efficient than anything else on the market."

Schlussler's Sun Frost refrigerators are made to run on 12 and 24 VDC, have the motors mounted on the top, and have four inches of insulation in places. The refrigerators are nonstandard sizes, so they don't always fit neatly into the spot in the kitchen designed for normal refrigerators. Baumgart paid $2,400 for his new DC electric Sun Frost refrigerator in 1984.

To power the refrigerator, Baumgart installed an array of four solar modules on his roof. His modules are Arco M75, rated at 40 watts each (ArcoSolar has since been purchased by Siemens, which has been purchased by Shell). In 1984, he paid $350 per module, which measure approximately 1 by 4 feet each.

His array of four solar modules charges a large deep-cycle marine battery that is protected from overcharge by a controller. The battery is wired to the Sun Frost refrigerator and has an automatic battery charger backup in the inverter. He uses the Trace inverter model #1512, 1.5 Kw, one of the first made by Trace in the mid-1980s. Though the refrigerator is designed to run from the power stored in the battery, when the battery is low, the inverter will kick in, pulling AC power from the grid to charge it. The refrigerator is therefore on a discrete system that is designed to access the grid when necessary. Baumgart plans to use the system to power some 12-volt lights when he increases his battery storage, as well as power a regular 110 VAC household power circuit using the inverter.

Asked if he would build the same system from scratch again, Baumgart responds, "Probably not. I simply couldn't build the same system now because the parts are not available anymore. But also, in 1984, when I was at the home of the president of ArcoSolar in Chatsworth, he showed me his system. He used two efficient little Sanyo refrigerators powered from his solar array. He was powering his less-costly refrigerators and putting the difference in the cost into extra solar modules. That makes a lot of sense."

BAUMGART 12V SYSTEM

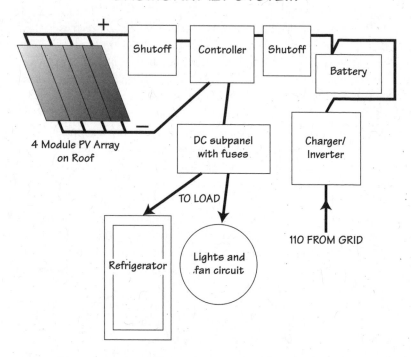

If you already have a properly sized solar electrical system, Baumgart suggests simply buying a highly efficient modern AC refrigerator as well as an extra solar module for your roof. He explains that one has to add to a system carefully, making sure the new module has the same ratings as the existing modules. "Buy an efficient AC refrigerator and get a sine wave inverter. . . . The modern sine wave inverters are highly efficient," he says.

"A lot of politicians say that this is not cost effective," Baumgart says with a smile. "Wrong! All this, including the refrigerator, has still cost me less than I would have paid for the grid power. My swimming pool solar array paid for itself in about seven years compared with what I would have paid to the power company in electricity. The refrigerator and solar array system purchase took longer for a payback, but I've never regretted spending $15 a month on electric bills for a pool and a 3,000-square-foot house."

His swimming pool solar array consists of six solar modules to power his backyard pool pump filter. He uses a 12-volt, ⅓ horsepower electric motor on a standard pool pump, which is directly powered by the six modules mounted on his fence; no battery is used. He doesn't use a solar-water heating system to heat the pool, but the pool's dark bottom absorbs some sunlight and keeps the water warmer than it would be if the bottom were white. At one time, he also used a plastic top cover composed of plastic bubbles designed to heat the water. "The cover actually overheated the water," says Baumgart, "so I don't use it." The cover is also a trapping and drowning hazard to children, pets, and suburban critters.

In general, modules may lose 10 percent of their electrical generating capacity over several decades. "So this system could outlive me," says Baumgart. He also points out that even if a system has lost 30 percent efficiency after several decades, which is highly doubtful, it is not necessary to fully replace the system. "You can add another module or two," says Baumgart. "But remember, it's not as easy as simply hooking up another module, although for the electrically inclined, it is done all the time. It has to be carefully sized to existing modules, which may not be available, so

POOL SYSTEM

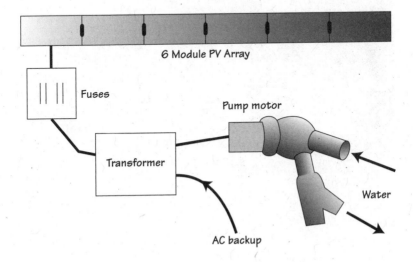

6 Module PV Array

Fuses

Pump motor

Transformer

Water

AC backup

resisters have to be added to balance the system. The smallest link in the chain of modules restricts the others to its output."

Baumgart recalls that back in 1954, when he was eight years old, he saw an advertisement in *National Geographic* magazine by Bell Laboratories. It said that solar cells could power the future, and that caught his attention and imagination. His family was very talkative, and everyone was aghast at the pollution they then experienced. He always wondered what was taking the government and industry so long to actually go solar.

"I'm not only an environmentally conscious person," he says, "I'm also a do-it-yourselfer. It galls me that I get a bill for something that I can do myself. It galls me that the power company sees me as a cow they can milk forever." He explains that he has no formal electrical background, having never taken an electrical or electronics class. "I just have a tinkerer's mind, and a copy of the *National Electrical Code* handbook. I never had to hire anyone to do any of this, and I never had any problems with my systems here."

Baumgart with the solar array that powers his pool pump.

He strongly recommends the *Real Goods Solar Living Source Book* to everyone, especially those who need a primer on how to plan a solar system and learn about the full range of appliances currently available.

"Visitors almost automatically ask me if I am off the grid," says Baumgart. He explains that he's not off the grid because he'd have to cut down too many trees that he loves. Living in an urban area, he believes that the future of solar is not just to go off the grid, but to find ways in which everyone can begin to supply at least *some* of their electricity via solar power, as he does.

"I feel a little closer to Mother Nature," says Baumgart about his conversion to solar power. "I didn't want to pollute, and I didn't like the way things were going, so this is what I had to do. Plus, I'm a lifelong do-it-yourselfer. This was not a choice for me. I *had* to do this."

The solar array that powers Baumgart's refrigerator and 12-volt system.

Baumgart next to his "power station."

Baumgart with his Sun Frost refrigerator.

Note the refrigerator's thick walls of insulation.

Profile 4: Eco-Home

Julia Russell is sitting in her living room talking to a small group who are participating in her Sunday tour. She is the founder of Eco-Home, a non-profit organization that grew from her concern for the future of her children and their health. She conducts regular tours of the home to show visitors what she and her group did to become a part of the energy solution. This particular Sunday, she tells the group how she would read *Organic Gardening* and *Mother Earth News* magazines to find healthful and sustainable ways to live.

"I came to realize that most of our environmental problems can be traced directly back to our modern urban lifestyle. I felt both overwhelmed and empowered, and I realized that I can change my own personal choices. I determined that I would find ways to use less of our natural resources, and I began with simple things," explained Russell. Some of the initial

Julia Russell shares her path to self-reliance at the beginning of an Eco-Home tour.

actions she took included using nontoxic cleaning products and recycling as much as possible.

Russell pauses and points to some Native American pictures on the walls, explaining that the original inhabitants of North America were masters at recycling and self-sustaining lifestyles. She adds that there are too many of us today to "live off the land" as the Native Americans did in the old days, but that a sustainable lifestyle is still possible if we learn how to use both science and technology in an intelligent manner, based upon ecological wisdom.

In addition to recycling, Russell also started xeriscaping—landscaping that requires less water—to help sustain her lifestyle. Instead of a lawn, there is a layer of tree leaf mulch. She rarely waters the area that was once a lawn, allowing it to remain cool and lush. The Eco-Home also has a gray water system whereby the used water goes through a simple particulate filter and is then pumped out to irrigate the fruit trees on the property.

She also educated herself about the manner in which electricity is generated. In the 1970s, she became aware of the coal-burning plants being built in the Four Corners area to provide electricity to southern California residents. "I felt that we had to go another way," she says, "so I chose to begin using the sun. About this time, the offer for a solar water heating system came up."

Russell explains the cycle of kitchen scraps to compost to new vegetables in her garden.

The 80-gallon tank storing solar-heated water on the left; the on-demand heater on the right..

From an Arizona company, she purchased three water-heating panels, which consisted of copper tubing on a flat panel. They came as a kit and cost about $800. She hired a plumber to install them on the roof.

This is known as an active system, which consists of a pump and solar panels that heat water stored in a heavily insulated 80-gallon tank in the basement. The tank is also connected to an on-demand heater—a device that heats water instantly—in case the water in the tank isn't hot enough. There is an intricate maze of copper pipes and shut-off valves involved in this system, so the do-it-yourselfer should thoroughly understand plumbing before attempting to install such a system.

Russell next considered how to utilize solar electricity; the Eco-Home now has two separate solar systems. The first is a stand-alone, off-the-grid system, which she hired an electrician to install in the 1980s. It consists of three small 45-watt panels, obtained second-hand, and six Trojan golf cart–type batteries. No inverter is needed in this system, but there is a controller. The 12 VDC from the batteries powers the ceiling quartz halogen lights in the kitchen and living room. Quartz halogen lights are more energy-efficient than incandescent bulbs.

Solar water heating panels above stand-alone 12-volt electrical system.

Russell shows the batteries for the 12-volt stand-alone PV system. The "controller" is shown on the left.

"This is a totally unique system that Rick Ulrich of Buel Solar installed," explains Russell. The stand-alone 12 VDC system is efficient, but it is all custom-made and the parts are now hard to get. "If I were to redo that today," says Ulrich, "I would just do it with 110-volt wiring and use a modern inverter."

Los Angeles's Department of Water and Power (DWP) installed the second solar system in 1998. At no cost to Russell, they installed a grid-connected 2-kilowatt system on her west-facing roof, where there is the maximum amount of sun in the afternoon. It consists of thirty-six panels, wired together in six large arrays. A Trace inverter is installed next to the meter, which actually goes backward when more power is produced than is used. Russell notes, however, that there is no accounting on her bill of the power generated compared with the power used. Still, she incurs no electric bills during the sunny season.

Russell's rooftop DWP-installed solar array.

Inverter for Russell's rooftop PV solar array.

This system was installed as a DWP program under the direction of David Freeman, who wanted to put solar electrical systems on Los Angeles residential roofs. Freeman explained that if the DWP could use 100,000 residential roofs to generate electricity, they would produce enough extra power to avoid having to build another power plant. The program allowed the DWP to install panels on the roofs of voluntary participants, and the power produced would then be fed back into the electrical grid. There would be no back-up power to the residents whose roofs were used and no reduction in their electrical bills. Participants would be required to maintain their own roof and allow DWP workers to come and go as needed for maintenance. The program was not popularly received and has since been discontinued.

Russell had the solar electrical system installed on her roof because she wanted visitors to her home to see what was possible and available. Based on the amount of electricity her roof system generated and the amount of power her home used during the day, she found that her home was completely powered by the sun during daylight hours.

On the Eco-Home tour, Russell explains that if you learn how to use natural lighting, you do not need to use electricity for that purpose. A light tube brings natural daylight into her kitchen during the day, making it unnecessary to turn on the lights.

As for cooking, Russell says, "We have no air conditioning here, so when we need to cook in the summer, we use a solar oven outside." Russell uses the popular Sun Oven, which can attain inside temperatures of up to 350 degrees F.

The house itself is energy efficient because the walls, ceiling, and floor are all well insulated. The windows are also double-glazed, and 3M film was put on the north-facing windows to reflect heat back into the room; the film is designed to reduce heat loss by as much as 26 percent. "I was able to tell the difference as soon as I put the film on the windows," says Russell.

Deciduous trees—trees that lose their leaves in winter—were planted along the west and south sides of the house to provide shade during the summer. The house was also built with overhanging eaves, which help provide summer shade.

Small gas-operated heaters are used for heating in the winter. A wood fireplace had been used previously some years ago, as Russell was able to prune the backyard fruit trees, let the cuttings dry, and use that in the woodstove. The wood ash was then also used on trees in the backyard. Russell stopped using the woodstove, however, after realizing that it was polluting the air.

"I'm a mother, and when I started being educated about the environmental problems our society is creating, I got concerned about whether we'd even have a planet for our children to be raised in," says Russell. "I had the opportunity to learn about our environment and our impact of modern life on our environment. I realized that our very lifestyle is the root of our environmental problems.

"So I decided to conduct an experiment. Could I modify my lifestyle so it would do less damage to the environment? Could I reduce my usage of natural resources? That was my goal, and I focused upon my personal lifestyle," explains Russell. "After several years of this, I saw the potential implications if millions were doing what I was doing. Now, I believe that is our only option for survival."

Russell's alternative to the internal combustion engine.

Russell's outreach program began in 1988 at a time when many environmental issues in the news had people horrified at the worldwide environmental damage. "We had a group of about ten of us, a core group that started the Eco-Home Network. We finished the systems that we do here, and we opened this home for tours in November of 1988."

Profile 5: Pioneers of Alternate Energy

The Forbes family of Sylmar, California, became alternate energy pioneers after the great Sylmar earthquake of 1971. Back then, Sylmar was one of the many communities nestled into the foothills of the Angeles National Forest in the northern section of Los Angeles County.

Ivan (left) and Glenn Forbes, true pioneers in alternate energy production, stand in front of part of their solar array.

The Forbeses felt the full impact of that quake, and subsequently had no electricity for about a week. The concept of solar power was just starting to trickle into the residential arena, and the modules available at the time lasted only a few years (they last at least twenty-five years today).

Because they had no gas after the earthquake, the family first installed an active hot water system using Libby/Owens/Ford solar water-heating panels and a pump. "It was an open-closed loop system," says Glenn Forbes. (The "open loop" part is not under city water pressure, whereas the "closed loop" is.)

At the time, the panels were one of the more expensive models available because they were made of copper plate and tubing with an aluminum frame. Libby/Owens/Ford panels are no longer manufactured. According to Glenn Forbes, the best domestic hot water panel available today would be either the Heliodyne or SunEarth models.

Like most homeowners, the Forbeses needed to hire plumbers and electricians to install and maintain various appliances. In this case, the solar water heater installers didn't do a good soldering job and didn't properly

Glenn stands in front of the solar water heating panels (solar PV panels on top, rear).

Glenn next to the solar water heating panels.

test their work—the system leaked. Once that was fixed, it operated flaw-lessly. Glenn Forbes says that most of the maintenance today requires checking components that could wear out and then fixing or replacing them.

The Forbes's fourteen water-heating panels use the sun to heat their water; the water is then pumped through a heat exchanger, which is con-nected to two 120-gallon water tanks. They also have a 220-volt backup connected to the house and a 600-gallon fiberglass tank for reserve and spa heating. This system provides plenty of hot water for ten months out of the year; only during two or more days of heavy rains is the electrical backup needed.

Hot water from the solar panels is stored here.

Even on an overcast day, the solar-heated water reaches over 100 degrees F.

FORBES'S SOLAR WATER HEATING

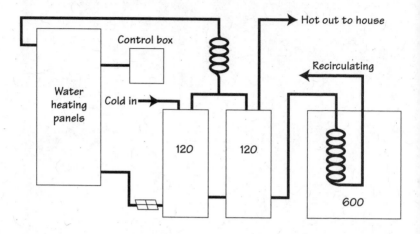

Vertical Access Wind Tower

Arising out of the Forbes's backyard, fully visible from the 210 Freeway some 10 feet beyond their fence, is a green towering object that remotely appears to be an industrial structure pertaining to the freeway. It's a vertical axis windmill, designed to generate electricity when the wind blows. The 42-foot tower was built and assembled by Glenn and friends, while his father, Ivan, secured permits and took care of other legal considerations.

Glenn Forbes had previous electrical experience from working in construction but says that the building of the tower was mostly "on-the-job training." His father adds, "The research and development on this device was such that we had the manufacturer build a three-stack unit to our custom specifications. Then we just put it together." Parts were preassembled, and the rest was bolted together in place with the aid of a crane.

Glenn and his father dug and poured a foundation to support the tower. It took 19 yards (42 tons) of concrete and rebar to create a 1-foot-thick slab over the three 4 by 4 by 8–foot deep pylons. The pylons would support the three 10-inch-thick oil casing pipes composing the framework for the three stacked vertical axis wind rotors. They considered using wooden telephone poles to support the wind-energy structure, but decided instead on metal pipes because they'd last longer and require less maintenance.

When the foundation was complete, Solar World (now defunct) delivered partially assembled parts, which Glenn and his father then installed.

With the three devices in place, stacked, and attached to a central shaft, the outside stators (stationary vertical blades) direct the wind into the blades driving the rotor, which in turn drives the alternator, creating the electrical current to be stored in the batteries.

Ivan Forbes conducted a wind study test at their site and found that the wind averaged about 7 mph, which would generally be considered below

The Forbes's vertical axis wind tower.

Glenn at the base of the vertical axis wind tower.

the threshold for a viable propeller-type wind system. Their vertical axis tower will turn with a wind of 3 mph, however, whereas most of the other products on the market will require about 15-plus mph. The tower is able to withstand high winds, although they will shut it down for safety reasons if the winds exceed 60 mph. The maximum rated output of this system is 12 kilowatts, which is seldom achieved, but the output is variable depending on wind conditions. The total estimated cost was approximately $20,000 in 1983. The type of wind turbine the Forbeses created hasn't been built since, but Glenn and Friends of the Wind Turbine are actively planning to build an up-to-date version using current technology. The new turbine will be approximately 40 feet tall, but it will not be

Another view of the vertical axis wind tower.

modular or in three sections. The plan is to have it built on-site with a small crew.

The Forbeses are the first residential cogenerators working with Los Angeles's Department of Water and Power. This means they are licensed to sell back "excess" power to the grid. For various "political" reasons, however, Glenn has removed the turbine from that status.

In addition to their wind turbine system, the Forbeses also have a stand-alone 5-kilowatt PV system. Their first solar electrical system included four used modules, rated at 30 watts and measuring 1 by 4 feet, which were wired to batteries to run their Sun Frost refrigerator. Their house burned down in 1997, however, and those first panels were lost. (According to

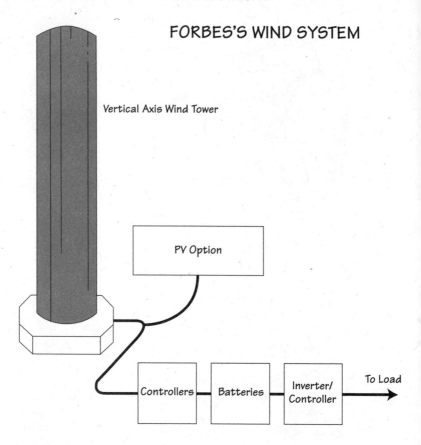

FORBES'S WIND SYSTEM

Vertical Axis Wind Tower

PV Option

Controllers — Batteries — Inverter/Controller

To Load

investigators, the Northridge earthquake created small holes in their attic and chimney, which ultimately led to their house fire two years later.)

They rebuilt the house with all-metal roofing for fire protection, and the entire solar array was set atop their solar greenhouse, separate from the house. The rebuilt house was insulated from top to bottom, and all the windows were dual-glazed. Heavy insulation means that less cooling is needed in the summer and less heat is needed in the winter. They also have a woodstove that provides almost 100 percent of their winter heating needs.

After they rebuilt from the fire, they obtained ten used 80-watt Krycera modules for approximately $200 each. They also purchased a Trace

(Xantrex) 2,400-watt inverter and C&D Liberty 2000 batteries (2-volt cells). They also obtained forty-two used modules, as well as six that were purchased new from solar author Joel Davidson.

They considered rebuilding the roof with the shingles that have the photovoltaic component built in, but according to Glenn Forbes, solar shingles are currently "only about half as efficient as the glass panel type. Such roofing shingles at this time have questionable durability. So, we will keep an eye on that technology until they can prove themselves."

After taking all these measures, they were able to get their electric bill down to $50 or less a month. However, they did not take the time to calculate the actual payback time of the solar panels and wind system. "We did this for fun and enjoyment," says Glenn. "We did the work ourselves and a lot of the components were used or gotten from salvage." They currently have a total of sixty-six PV modules, each generating 75 watts, for a total of a 5,000-plus wattage system.

Glenn shows the wiring from the PV array before it gets to the "power room."

A view of the Forbes's inverters.

FORBES'S PV SYSTEM

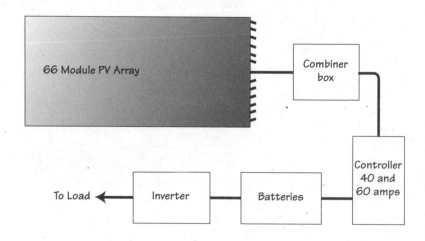

Glenn explains that you can mix and match any PV panels. They are usually wired in-line, called strings, and the life span is at least twenty-five years. All panels should be tested on a volt meter first to determine whether or not the panel is still usable.

Batteries

"We were on a tight budget, but in the early days I knew a guy who changed out batteries from a repeater station, and these were adequate for our needs. The cost was right, too—they were free," says Glenn with a smile. "They were sealed, so maintenance was easy. Later, I salvaged forty-four 8-volt flooded-type 500-pound storage batteries, which required a lot of maintenance. Years later, I found a Bob at Coast Energy Corp., and I was able to obtain forty-eight used 177-lb AGM batteries [sealed gel]. All batteries are heavy and require a high degree of caution since the high amperage is dangerous. You can expect about ten to fifteen years of life from a used battery and even more with new batteries if they're not abused.

Part of the Forbes's battery bank.

"Our power usage is pretty constant, so all we've had to do over the past twenty years is tweak our system," explains Glenn. "We've had no negative reactions from anyone regarding our system or what we do. In fact, lots of people from all over the world have stopped by over the past twenty years to look at our system. Back in 1993, Real Goods started the first tours of Energy Independent homes, and they put us on the tour."

PROBLEMS AND CHALLENGES

Many components that you can purchase today have been perfected to the point where you simply don't have the same problems you may have encountered in the past, but you still have to take the time to check and maintain your system.

Perhaps one of the biggest problems today is the possibility of hiring someone to install an electrical system who doesn't know what he's doing. Electricians' biggest problem tends to be not following the National Electrical Code (NEC) guidelines, section 690. There is no permit required to install a PV system under 50 volts, but it's a good idea to get a certified installer who will obtain a permit and do a good job. You will need a permit if you decide on a grid-connected system. More information can be found through the American Solar Energy Society (ASES) at www.ases.org or through *Homepower* magazine at www.homepower.com.

"Remember," adds Glenn, "most of this is easy if you take your time and realize that now you are responsible to be your own power company. This is not something you install and then just forget about. We know someone who put forty-eight panels on his roof through some rebate deal. The panels were on the roof for three years, but he did nothing to clean the panels and never checked the inverter or batteries. The inverter was in a cabinet with no circulation, was improperly installed, and eventually burned out."

RECOMMENDATIONS

The Forbeses recommend that others get started on the path to self-sufficiency by first installing a domestic solar water heating system. "A $3,000 investment can save you 80 percent on your heating bill," says Glenn.

Installing a PV and battery system is the next step. You can buy, add, or build according to the growth of your needs. Conduct an energy survey to determine your energy needs. Your power bill shows your daily and monthly usage, so this is a good place to start. Glenn suggests you "start by producing enough power so you can have lights, especially when there is a blackout and there's no power. Then expand from there. You can consider adding a small gas or diesel generator to use as backup also. Make sure the inverter you choose will start the generator."

The Forbeses do not recommend that people go out and purchase 12-volt appliances, such as those that are sold to the recreational vehicle market. RV appliances are generally found to be inferior compared with their 110-volt counterparts. They suggest that you install a PV system, run the battery power through an inverter, and then use 110- and 240-volt appliances.

Although their first big energy-saving adventure was in using wind power, they wouldn't recommend that for beginners. Wind devices are a bit more complex, and there may also be local zoning law restrictions. Glenn says that neighbors, moreover, are more likely to complain about wind devices than solar devices.

For solar water heating, they recommend an Australian manufacturer of solar water heating panels, SolaHart (www.solahart.websyte.com.au). Glenn suggests getting two or three panels and an 80-gallon storage tank with gas, propane, or electrical backup.

A rainwater catchment tank is also a good idea. Glenn has a 250-gallon tank next to the greenhouse for emergency irrigation and other uses.

5

SOLAR
WATER HEATING

Two primary factors fueled the interest in solar water heating systems in the 1970s: the energy crisis with higher oil prices expected, and the 50 percent tax credits. According to solar installer Mike Butler, when the credits were stopped in 1985 and oil prices didn't skyrocket, most of the companies who'd been in the business of installing solar water heaters took on other work or went out of business

Is it viable to heat our everyday water with the sun? Anyone who has tried to drink water from a hose on a hot day knows that the water can sometimes be *too* hot to drink, and you'd need to let the hose run for a few minutes to flush it of hot water. This example demonstrates how easily the sun can heat water.

SOLAR SHOWER

The Stearns SunShower (and its many imitations) employs solar energy to heat enough water for one or two showers. To use the shower, you simply fill a heavy-duty plastic bag and place it in the sun for an hour or until the water is hot. You then hang the bag in a nearby tree and take your hot shower outdoors. Such showers are good for camping trips or in the aftermath of a hurricane or earthquake when there is no conventional hot water.

Once, when my water main broke, I had to rely on stored water for two days. Realizing my predicament, I filled my SunShower and laid it out in the sun. When I needed to bathe three hours later, I took a wonderful hot shower under the grapefruit tree. I have since taken my solar shower device on numerous camping trips and day trips into the woods. It has never ceased to amaze me that I am able to shower with water heated solely by the sun, without the need for fire, propane, or other fuels. But a solar shower is not going to be your ideal alternate choice for regularly heating water in your urban home. Let's therefore explore some other options.

THE BREADBOX

My first serious experiment in solar water heating took place in the late 1970s. I found a gas water heater that someone had discarded on trash day. I was told that the cast iron tank still held water, so I removed the outer sheet metal shell and fiberglass and took the tank home. I cleaned it out, spray-painted it black, and plumbed it so it could receive a garden hose at the inlet and another garden hose at the drain.

It was summertime, so I set the tank on a 55-gallon drum next to our outside bathtub. I filled it with water early in the day. By sunset, I let the water drain into my bathtub for a hot bath—the temperature measured about 100 degrees Fahrenheit. It was wonderful. Had I been out camping, I would have considered this an amazing luxury. But unless you really enjoy taking outside baths or showers during the day or you simply have no other choice, this sort of bathing gets tiresome after a while. And once the sun goes down, your 100-degree water will cool off quickly.

To improve upon this simple system and keep the water hot longer, you might construct a solar water heating "breadbox," also called a batch heater. I decided to build an insulated box around that same black water heater tank. The resulting breadbox allowed the water to absorb heat during the day without losing all its heat at night.

A few basic principles explain the breadbox's effectiveness. Heat from the sun causes the water to expand. Cold water is denser and therefore heavier than hot water. This means that the hotter water in your tank will be at the top, and the colder water will be at the bottom. When cold water is introduced into the bottom of the tank, it forces the hot water out of the top exit pipe. Some mixing occurs, so you are usually not able to take advantage of all the hot water in the tank. There is less mixing with an upright tank, however, than there is with a horizontal tank.

I've seen many different types of breadbox water heaters. Some have the water tank standing upright and others have the tank lying horizontally.

Though upright is the best option to eliminate cold and hot water mixing, it is a challenge to safely support a 400-plus-pound box leaning back at a 45-degree angle—unless, of course, it is simply "leaning" on your roof. The horizontal tank is easier to construct and has little danger of falling over, but there is a greater temperature loss due to the way in which the hot and cold water will mix.

When I took all these factors into account and considered my location, my skills, and my budget, I chose to build a horizontal breadbox. I have included some of the construction details here. I will attempt to explain the basic details of constructing both types of breadboxes. The illustration on page 120 should also help you visualize the construction as you read through the instructions.

Start by assembling the end pieces. If you build a triangular box that will lie flat (as I did), you start with a 48 by 48–inch piece of plywood, at least ½ inch thick. Cut it diagonally. If you choose to build a rectangular, upright breadbox, the two end pieces will measure 24 by 48 inches each. On the inside of each of the end pieces, screw or nail another piece of plywood that has an involute curve cut into it. This is used to create a reflector to cast more light onto the water tank.

Using two-by-fours and standard carpentry techniques, attach the two end pieces to create the skeleton for your box. The inside of the box should be at least one foot longer than the tank. You will need to leave room for insulation and plumbing attachments. Nail or screw a plywood back and bottom to the triangular box, or plywood back and sides to the rectangular box.

Before you insulate the box, you will need to drill the necessary holes. My triangular box needed six holes—one for the water inlet, one for the hot water outlet, and four for the two 2-inch galvanized pipes, which were suspended through the box by two holes in each end. These pipes support the 400-pound tank, though you could also use angle iron bolted to each inside end.

The next step is to insulate the inside of the box. You can use sheet Styrofoam from a lumber yard or whatever else may be available. I used old acoustical tiles because I had a free and abundant source of them. They may not have been the best insulator in the end, but that's what my budget allowed.

Next, you'll measure some flexible cardboard and tack it from end piece to end piece for each of the involute curves; this will form your two reflective surfaces. Fill the hollow cavity (beneath the cusp) with fiberglass insulation or other insulating material such as Styrofoam cups or egg cartons. Attach tin foil or sheets of reflective Mylar to the entire inside surface of the box. Rubber cement works well for this step, as do various spray-on adhesives. All seams should then be caulked to prevent leakage.

You can now set your water tank onto the two support pipes and attach the plumbing. Once that's completed, fill the tank with water and check for leaks. No leaks? Good! (If there *are* leaks, tighten things up before proceeding.) Cover the box with either clear plastic or, even better, one or more glass doors.

I built the triangular design, so I first experimented by simply setting the breadbox on two 55-gallon drums. In order to take a bath or shower, I'd just let the water drain out. That worked okay, to a point. When I attached the hose so the cold water would force out the hot water, there seemed to be little very hot water because of the mixing of the two temperatures, which was never fully corrected due to the inefficiencies of a horizontal tank.

Many people in remote areas use similar solar water heaters, which work well on sunny days. To eliminate heat loss at night, an insulated door can be added. If you choose to install one of these, you will need to close the door each night and open it every morning, which may seem like a lot of maintenance. If your batch water heater is on your roof, you won't want to open and close doors every day. The next best solution is to simply add a double- or even triple-walled glass door to the front of the heater.

The most common way to integrate a solar water heater with a home's existing gas heating system is to have the breadbox serve as a preheating device for the gas heater. You would route the incoming cold water first through the solar water heater, then send the heated water back into your gas water heater before it travels to your sink or bathtub. As long as the sun heats the water enough, your gas heater will not turn on. If you install such a system, make sure to completely insulate the hot water line from the solar water heater to the gas water heater. If you don't, heat will be lost along the entire length of the pipe, resulting in an inefficient system.

MAKING A BATCH SOLAR WATER HEATER

Drawing the cusp shape onto triangular or rectangular plywood

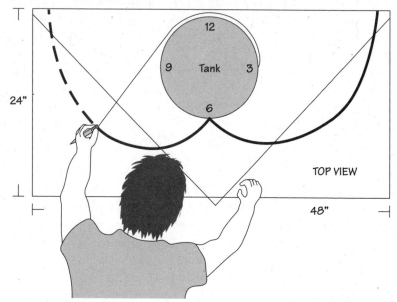

24"

12

9 Tank 3

6

TOP VIEW

48"

Stand tank on plywood. Attach a pencil to a string and secure that string to the 3 o'clock position of the tank. The pencil should reach just to the 6 o'clock position. As you unwind the string, the curve is drawn. Reverse for the opposite side.

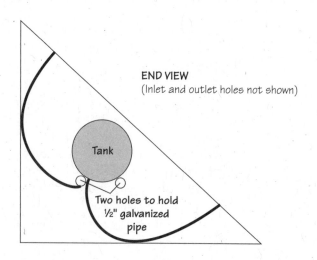

END VIEW
(Inlet and outlet holes not shown)

Tank

Two holes to hold
½" galvanized
pipe

BATCH SOLAR WATER HEATERS

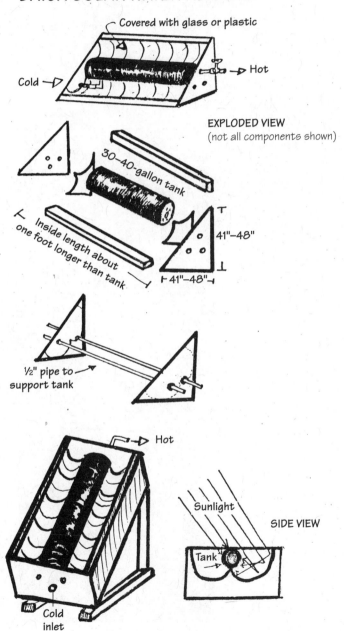

Covered with glass or plastic

Cold →

→ Hot

EXPLODED VIEW
(not all components shown)

30–40-gallon tank

Inside length about one foot longer than tank

41"–48"

41"–48"

½" pipe to support tank

→ Hot

Sunlight

SIDE VIEW

Tank

Cold inlet

Suzy Beale checks out the framework for the breadbox.

The tank has been placed into the framework.

Depending on the alignment of your breadbox and your conventional water heater, you might also lose heat at night if warm water from the gas heater circulates to the breadbox, especially if the breadbox is not well insulated. You should install a check valve, which is a one-way valve designed to stop reverse thermosiphoning at night.

Another consideration when plumbing a breadbox heater into an existing gas system is where you place it in relation to the gas heater. Keep in mind that hot water rises, so if your breadbox is *above* the gas water heater, the water in the breadbox will get hot; if the breadbox is not well insulated, however, it can lose that heat at night.

An ideal configuration is to situate the breadbox heater *below* your conventional water heater. As the water in the breadbox heats, it will rise into the gas water heater. If the temperature in the gas heater stays high, the gas will not turn on. When I built my breadbox, I lived on a steep north-facing hill, and there simply was no "below" where I could place

Beale examines the tank.

Plastic is used to cover this breadbox, but glass is more efficient.
JANICE FRYLING

The finished breadbox.
JANICE FRYLING

the breadbox. The roof was so steep, moreover, that it was out of the question to place it up there. The breadbox solar water heater therefore became a fascinating conversation piece, and I enjoyed many wonderful hot baths under the stars.

I built my first breadbox solar water heater for about $78, when most "experts" were saying I'd need to spend from $500 to $600. If a person were to buy all the materials new, it may have been possible to spend that amount. I, however, was able to use scrap materials and odd supplies I had lying around the homestead. Breadbox solar water heaters are believed to be the cheapest solar water heaters to build and cost the least to produce or save one BTU. Although the breadbox is generally not considered to be the most efficient system, if you are on a very modest budget, a breadbox heater will still provide you with a basic way to heat water using the sun.

PROFESSIONAL INSTALLATION

We had always wanted a "professional" solar water heating system, but the cost was prohibitive. We then got to know Michael Butler of Solar Performance, who was a professional installer and maintainer of solar systems. (Currently, he only does repair and maintenance of solar systems.) Since 1984, he's installed more than five hundred solar water heating systems on southern California roofs. You can imagine our joy when he called us one winter day to ask if we wanted a free solar water heating panel and the insulated tank to go with it. One of his former customers was installing a new roof, and rather than take down the solar system and replace it when the roof was done, she asked Butler to simply dispose of it.

He brought it over the next day and gave me some written instructions on how to install it. I read the instructions carefully and asked many questions. I felt I could handle the job, but I didn't want to spend weeks installing it only to encounter leaks and other problems. Deep down, I knew I'd eventually be calling Butler to have him install the system. After all, he'd already installed *hundreds* of solar water-heating systems and knew the answers to the questions before I even asked them. A year later, in 1999, I finally called Butler and arranged for him to install the system, which took a total of two days.

On the first day, Butler went into the attic to "beef up" the ceiling rafters. No one wants a 400-plus-pound tank to drop through the roof into the bedroom. Butler measured everything carefully and placed two extra two-by-fours in the ceiling directly under where the new tank would be. He then built a redwood frame to hold the tank on the roof and another frame to hold the solar collector panel. After those steps were finished, Butler and I carried up the empty insulated tank to the roof and placed it into position. We then carried up the panel and put it into position, and Butler connected the two pieces. The panel was lighter than the tank but more difficult to carry because of its awkward size. The following day, Butler installed all the copper pipes to make the system work. The solar system was passive, so it was plumbed to be a preheater for both of our home's water heaters.

Professional solar installer Mike Butler secures a wooden frame to the roof. The frame will hold the tank of solar-heated water.

Butler and Nyerges carrying the solar water heater onto the roof.

Passive Systems

A solar water heating system can be either passive or active. Passive means that there is no pump to move the water around, and the water tank is typically mounted above the water heating panels. (See the illustration on page 134 to see how our system was put together.)

An active system involves a pump, which is a bit more complicated. The advantage to this system is that you do not have to mount a heavy water tank on your roof (see illustration on page 135). As of this writing, about 95 percent of professionally installed solar systems are active.

The exact details will vary from house to house, but the following explains what Butler did to our roof. Where the incoming cold water would normally go into the gas water heater, the water was instead sent into the solar panel for heating. From there, the water is heated and fills the attached tank. When we turn on the hot water at the sink, the pressure forces the water back into the gas water heater, through the entire system, and finally comes out the tap in the kitchen or bathroom. As long as the sun has heated the water adequately, the gas heater does not turn on. The

Butler on the roof.

Butler checks the inlet and outlet valves on the back of the water tank. Note the outlet hot water lines, insulated in white foam.

hot water lines leading from the solar water heater to the gas heaters were completely insulated.

There is a possibility that the solar-heated water could get *too* hot, so Butler installed a thermostat on a mixing valve just before the solar-heated water enters the gas water heater. Should the incoming water be too hot (which could actually damage the gas heater), some cold water will mix with it to bring the temperature down.

On the first full day that the system was working, we felt the pipes that were full of the solar-heated water. They were quite hot—Butler smiled broadly as he checked out the system. "You're in the solar age now!" he exclaimed.

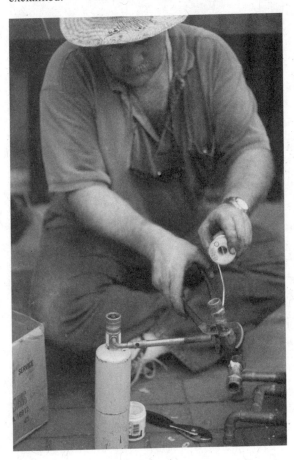

Butler welds some of the copper components.

A view of the valve that needed to be added. This valve causes the incoming cold water to first go through the solar system, then into the gas water heater, before it comes out the tap inside the house. If the sun keeps the water hot, the gas water heater does not turn on. The handle at middle right is a bypass valve if it becomes necessary to turn off the flow of water through the solar water heater. This valve is used when repairs are necessary to either the solar system or the gas water heater.

The finished solar water heater system.

Close-up view of the finished system. Afternoon shadows never seemed to affect the system's overall efficiency.

COMMERCIAL SOLAR SYSTEMS

There are still plenty of commercial solar water heating systems available. Knowing exactly what you need before you make a purchase will help you choose the best system for your situation. When you see water heating systems in catalogs, keep in mind that the cost doesn't include installation. You can either install the system yourself or hire someone to do it for you; installation therefore needs to be factored into your projected cost.

We have regularly seen used solar water heaters advertised in the classified sections of local newspapers. In the two times we spoke with the sellers, both had similar situations. One was reroofing in preparation for a house sale and didn't want to pay to reinstall the system. The other person was selling a condominium and didn't want any complications to hold up the sale. She was the only one in her entire complex with such a system, and there was a complication within the homeowners' association regarding the solar heater. To simplify her sale, she simply had it removed.

No matter when you choose to produce your own power, there will be problems and obstacles to overcome. This is true for solar water heating, photovoltaics, wind power, methane, and so on. Each system requires that you educate yourself about the necessary operations and maintenance requirements before installing it. "Freedom from the grid" is therefore never free.

We think producing some of your own power is the right choice, nevertheless, and making such a decision is good for the long-term health of the planet.

Although you cannot tell the difference from water heated by the sun versus water heated by gas, we enjoy letting the sun heat our water. That may not seem like a tangible benefit (such as saving money), but it's still a very real benefit to us.

BUTLER'S ADVICE

Butler explains that the average homeowner wanting to get into the solar age must first decide between a passive and an active solar water heating system.

Passive

The passive systems do not use a pump, and the water tank is situated above the water heating panels. These systems are the easiest to install for the do-it-yourselfer who has a basic knowledge of plumbing. The only passive system that Butler recommends is manufactured by CopperHeart. "The system by CopperHeart will cost about $1,700 for a 40-gallon system," says Butler, "plus the cost, or time, needed to install it." The most common use of a breadbox heater is to have it act as a preheater for a conventional water heating system.

Active

"Nearly all the solar water heating systems being installed today are active systems," says Butler. Active systems have a pump that forces the hot water through the system, and the water tank can be positioned at ground level instead of on the roof. Butler recommends a Grundfos pump with a GL30 controller. The tank should be one manufactured specifically for use in a solar system. "A do-it-yourselfer could take an electric water heating tank and make that work, if he knows what he's doing," says Butler.

He doesn't recommend a particular brand of heating panels, but he does suggest obtaining a standard water heating panel with copper tubing and ½-inch risers. The panel should either be painted black or, even better, made of black chrome. The latter costs more but is 5 percent more efficient. American Rheen manufactures good panels for solar water heating systems.

Untrained individuals should not try to install their own active systems. "Most people who are trying to save money do not do this correctly, because even if they are good plumbers, they often do not know the parts and concepts that are strictly solar," says Butler. He suggests calling a licensed solar contractor to get references; the best way to find a good solar contractor is to talk to the people who have had it done and see how they liked the service.

Be sure that the solar installer uses only equipment that is certified by the Solar Rating and Certification Corporation (SRCC). Any commercially made solar system should be rated by the SRCC. The International

PASSIVE SOLAR WATER HEATING

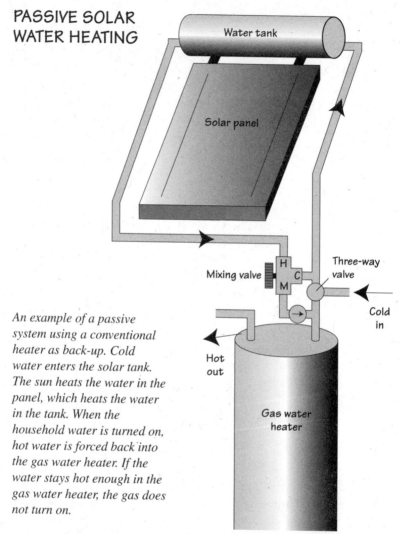

Water tank

Solar panel

Mixing valve

H C
M

Three-way valve

Cold in

Hot out

Gas water heater

An example of a passive system using a conventional heater as back-up. Cold water enters the solar tank. The sun heats the water in the panel, which heats the water in the tank. When the household water is turned on, hot water is forced back into the gas water heater. If the water stays hot enough in the gas water heater, the gas does not turn on.

A three-way valve where the water first enters the system allows the solar system to be shut down for repairs while the conventional gas heater continues to provide hot water for the household. Also, there is a tempering—or mixing—valve that contains a thermostat. If the water coming in from the solar panel is too hot, cold water will mix with it before it enters the gas water heater tank.

ACTIVE SOLAR WATER HEATING

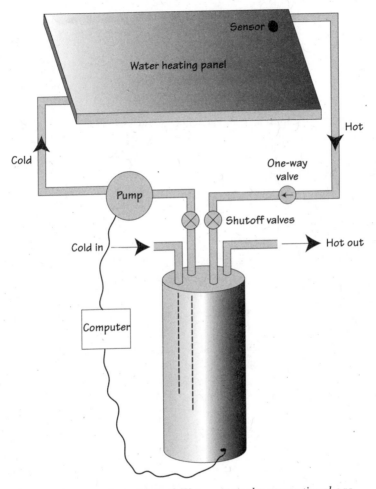

There is no heavy tank on the roof. Water enters the conventional gas water heating tank, and a pump moves water into the lower end of the panel. The sun heats the water, and it is forced out and back into the tank. A computer attached to sensors will shut off the pump on a very hot day if the tank gets too hot.

Another possibility with an active system is a heat exchange tank that contains antifreeze.

Association of Plumbing and Mechanical Officials (IAPMO) is also a reputable organization. According to Butler, "Any plumbing or mechanical items must have IAPMO approval before being sold to the public. It is best to avoid purchasing any systems not approved by the IAPMO or SRCC." For more information on either of these organizations, visit www.solar-rating.org or www.iapmo.org.

Maintenance

On a passive system, less maintenance is required. Three types of safety valves must be kept in good working order: the freeze valve, the temperature and pressure (TNP) valve, and the tempering valve (also known as the mixing valve, which mixes cold water with the hot solar water when the latter gets too hot). These valves should be rebuilt every five years or so. Otherwise, the homeowner only needs to periodically check the system to make sure there are no leaks and the lines bringing in hot solar water are staying hot.

Butler also suggests hiring a professional solar contractor to do a regular checkup. Whereas leaks are easy to see, other problems may not be apparent for years. "The pump might stop working so water won't circulate, or the conventional water heater connected to the solar system might have gone bad. I've actually seen systems like this where the homeowner had no idea their system was not working," says Butler. A professional contractor will spot potential problems long before the system stops working, which is why Butler strongly recommends that you have a professional solar contractor regularly check your active system.

PURCHASING MATERIALS

You will most likely purchase your tank and solar panels from a manufacturer. For the vast majority of us, it is a far more efficient use of our time and money to purchase manufactured components than try to make them ourselves. What you might construct from scrap and spare parts would make an entertaining article for *Mother Earth News*, but it could also take a long time to put together and result in a far less efficient system than a professional. It therefore becomes necessary to purchase parts, so we must be able to trust both the sellers of the parts and the installers.

SLOPPY INSTALLATION

Solar installer Alan Robert has encountered the following problems
with companies that incorrectly install solar systems:

- Insulation on the hot water pipes not taped or glued on, or no insulation at all
- Extension cords run through the walls
- Water heater shed wobbly and not properly sealed
- Equipment on a north roof where it doesn't get any sun
- Equipment in a shady area
- Valves turned the wrong way
- Wood racks (that hold the tank) not painted
- Roof structures not internally reinforced
- Installation is sloppy, ugly, and unappealing
- Roof leaks where solar system is attached (either not caulked, or done quickly and insufficiently)
- Pumps installed in the wrong direction
- Pipes run to the wrong place
- Work not done to local building and safety codes

**"Why is it that we never have the time to do a job right the
first time, but we can always find the time to fix it later?"**

—Dave Hereford

Dishonest Tactics

Alan Robert, a solar installer who spent years in the industry, alerted me
to some of the dishonest and misleading tactics some solar companies
may use.

"I have heard all of the following used by solar water heating and solar
electricity salesmen," says Robert. "They will tell you that the system will
supply *all* of your electric or hot water needs. This is rarely the case, and
the salesmen tend to not discuss that the average system cannot supply
100 percent of your needs under all circumstances. They will tell you that

your south roof will get thirteen hours of sun, and your west roof will get eight hours of sun. This is probably not so, but even if it is, it is usually not all *usable* light, and the actual usable hours will be about half that."

Robert explains that sometimes the installers will simply install what you are willing to pay for, and the resulting system may be too small to be practical or useful. "They would rather sell you something than sell you nothing," he says, "so you really want to do your homework first so you know what you need, as well as what equipment will fill that need."

"Often, the solar installers will promise to remove and reinstall your entire system if you have to put on a new roof. You better get this promise in writing," advises Robert. "The promise means nothing if the company goes out of business, however. And going out of business is pretty common in this industry. Another sales tactic is to tell you that your system— either solar water or PV—is maintenance free. Nothing is maintenance free."

According to Robert, 90 percent of all the systems he has examined have one or more of the problems listed on page 137. "These are all avoidable problems, and the solar installer should know the building codes and follow them," he says. "The installer should take the time to install the system well and test it before departing."

The root problem is that the installers are in a rush because the quicker they finish the job, the more they earn per hour. "Unfortunately, too many of the guys who did solar installing took no pride in their work and just rushed from job to job," says Robert. "Then, when there were problems with the installation, they had already gone out of business and were probably somewhere else installing screen doors or selling insurance."

EQUIPMENT FLAWS

Problems with the equipment itself can also cause a system to work improperly. Never buy a water heating panel that has copper risers less than ½ inch in diameter. Smaller risers can clog up with calcium, sand, and other miscellaneous gunk, and they are more likely to freeze in the winter due to poor circulation.

Overly complex systems should also be avoided. A drain-down system, for example, will shut off the valves if it senses that the system is freezing, and then begin circulating when the temperature is higher.

"The more complex system you have, the greater likelihood you have for problems," says Robert. "Though the drain-down system may sound like a good idea, in actual practice it requires much more maintenance. It is much better to use a heat-exchange system if you live in a very cold environment."

Some solar systems use dissimilar metals within the unit, which causes the metals to break down. "When you buy equipment, or if someone else is buying it for you, be sure to ask about this," advises Robert.

The ideas presented in this chapter are just a few of the many ways in which we can attempt to use solar power to provide our needed hot water for bathing, washing, and cooking. These are by no means, however, the only methods. For more information on solar water heating, see the resources section on page 257.

6

WATER IS
THE KEY TO LIFE

Throughout history, towns and villages have sprung up near water sources; every major city in the world began near a water source. Only within the last century have population growth and new technologies allowed us to create cities where the local land itself cannot support the vast numbers of people now residing there.

Los Angeles is such a city. The movie *Chinatown* gives viewers a fairly accurate picture of what was needed to bring water to the southern California coastal desert plain so that real estate developers could begin parceling up the otherwise arid land.

Palm Springs is another such anomaly—home to the rich and famous, land of a million golf courses, land that nature did not intend for expanses of grass. It seems that the planners of Palm Springs don't understand that they live smack in the middle of an arid desert where cacti and tortoises were intended to thrive, where their green lawns only survive because of the profligate waste of precious water. Those who wish to be a part of the ecologic solution must always take water use into account.

If you live in an urban or suburban area, your water most likely comes to you from local sources, and you pay your local water company to supply you with safe water. In some cases, the water is not local and it must travel hundreds of miles to get to you. Los Angeles gets the majority of its water from hundreds of miles away. It makes sense if you live in any such area that you analyze your water use, discover your local water sources, and take the steps necessary to conserve water.

OUR WATER USAGE

If you intend to store water for emergencies, you should first measure your actual water usage. Record the amount you use per day, then multiply it by the amount of people in your household. You might be surprised to see how much you actually use. And don't forget occasional water uses, such as cleaning countertops or irrigating.

You should store enough water to last you for about two weeks. In an emergency, your water use would most likely be limited to the bare essentials as follows:

- Drinking (humans, pets, and farm animals)
- Bathing and hygiene
- Preparing food
- Watering vegetable gardens

Containers used for water storage.

BE AWARE OF LOCAL SOURCES

Swimming Pools

In urban areas, swimming pools could be an emergency water source if supplies were suddenly cut off. A swimming pool cannot be considered a permanent way to supply your water unless it is fed by a spring or other natural source.

A swimming pool still contains a few hundred gallons of water, which would last a long time in an emergency. In the movie *Hotel Rwanda*, residents of a hotel where the water is shut off by the military have no other

A swimming pool is a good source of emergency water.

water source except the swimming pool. They use the swimming pool's water for washing and bathing, as well as for cooking and food preparation. The most hazardous complication about using normal swimming pool water is the chlorine used to keep it clean. In order to use swimming pool water, no chemical contaminants (other than chlorine, which is already found in urban tap water) should be present. To kill off any biological contaminants, however, one only needs to boil the water.

Wells

Wells are essentially just holes in the ground; there are, however, countless ways in which to dig those holes. A hole is usually dug in a low location where underground water is likely to be found. One may seek the assistance of a geologist or a dowser to locate a well site.

The well can simply be an old-fashioned pit lined with rocks where a bucket is drawn upward with the water. Or the well can be large and have steps you walk down to collect water.

Modern wells are a different matter, however, and they all require electric pumps that can be operated by solar-produced electricity.

Rain

Rain is perhaps the most overlooked source of water in arid regions. As little as a century ago, rainwater collection systems were far more common than they are today. In such systems, rainwater is essentially collected in buckets or cisterns. Studies have determined that this is a viable way to obtain at least some of one's needed annual water. The two primary limiting factors are the amount of roof space and the number of storage containers available.

I have collected as many as 400 gallons of water in a single storm simply by placing buckets (small and large) around the house where the water streamed off the awnings. When the smaller, 5-gallon buckets were full, I poured the water into the larger 30- and 40-gallon buckets. When the larger buckets were full, I covered them so mosquitoes would not breed.

If you plan to collect rainwater on a regular basis, a metal roof works best so sand and asphalt residue do not continually flow into your water. (This may not be a serious concern if you plan to use the water entirely for agriculture, washing, and outside applications.) If a metal roof is too costly, you may also consider a rubberized coating for a standard three-tab asphalt shingle roof. I covered my roof with a white product made by Henry that is generally used to reduce the heat in a home's attic. It helps seal any small roof leaks and gives the roof a slick white surface to facilitate rainwater collection.

One must also take into consideration the weight of water, which is roughly 8 pounds per gallon. This means that although a 5-gallon bucket can be moved about relatively easily (at approximately 40 pounds), a 30-gallon bucket will weigh about 240 pounds and will most likely stay where it is for months until the water is used.

You should therefore carefully consider the placement of your rain-collecting buckets. A house, barn, or garage with rain gutters is ideal for harvesting rain water. All the rain hitting the roof will generally funnel down to the downspouts, where it can then be directed into containers of whatever size you choose. If you build your own collection container, be sure to plan an overflow valve as the amount of rain you collect in a single storm might be far more than you expected.

USING RAIN BARRELS

While driving up a beautiful Pasadena street lined with tall deodar trees, I was admiring the bungalow houses with their well-kept gardens and trees. I suddenly saw something unexpected at one of the houses (although it should be common at every home): the downspout at the southwest corner drained into a rain barrel!

I pulled over to get a better look. The barrel was large and made of plastic, similar to the type I'd seen used to import pickles into the United States. The entire lid could be screwed off to gain access to the water. The top had been modified with a screen to remove debris that came down from the roof, and a spigot had been added to the bottom so one could easily use the collected rain water. I wanted to see the barrel up close, so I walked up to the house and met the owner, Carol Kampe, who was working in her yard. She happily gave me a tour of her rain collection system.

As it turned out, she had a total of ten rain-collecting barrels strategically located to collect the most rain possible from the house and garage roofs. Two of the barrels held 65 gallons each; the other eight held 60 gallons each. The rain she collects is used for outdoor purposes only, such as watering her fruit trees and other plants in the yard.

"Generally, I have enough rainwater in my barrels to last me until August," says Kampe. She is therefore able to rely on the rain for watering her yard for approximately two-thirds of the year. Kampe estimates that she saves perhaps $300 a month in payments to the water company.

"But I don't do this for economic reasons," Kampe adds. "I do it because we live in a desert here in southern California. Water will become more critical as time goes on. So it is just a shame to waste all this good rain."

Kampe had been living in her home for just a few years when she decided to purchase seven of the rain-collecting barrels. She has since

Rain flowing off the roof into Kampe's rainwater collection barrels. Note the smaller white pipe, which is an overflow line for yard irrigation. Some of her barrels are also daisy-chained so that as one barrel fills, the overflow begins to fill the next barrel.

added three more. The barrels were purchased for about $100 each from a company that modifies the pickle barrels into rain-collecting barrels. The company also provides hoses so the barrels can be "daisy-chained," allowing the overflow of one barrel to fill the other barrels. The lids of the rain barrels can also be unscrewed in order to scoop out water as needed for individual plants.

When planning a rain-collecting system such as this, one has to therefore understand that the full barrel cannot be moved. One may instead connect other barrels to the barrel under the downspout so that the overflow can be collected in a spot away from the house.

Another Kampe rain barrel. Note the spigot toward the bottom for emptying or attaching a hose.

Rain flows from the gutters and passes through a screen before filling the barrel.

Kampe laughed at all the current talk about "living green" as if it were something new. "We were doing all this back in the 1970s," she says, describing how she used to recycle and collect rain in her former home of Indiana. Emphasizing the need to save and conserve water in regards to ever-increasing populations, Kampe echoes George Santayana in saying that "anyone who doesn't learn from history is doomed to repeat it."

Her home has all compact flourescent lights (CFL), which last about five times as long as conventional incandescent bulbs and use about one-quarter the energy. She also has light tubes that direct sunlight into the house, meaning that she doesn't need to use electricity for lighting during the day. Although she considered photovoltaic solar electricity and solar water heating systems, the alignment of her house as well as the abundance of nearby trees makes such systems less than ideal.

TREEPEOPLE CATCHES SOME RAIN

Founded by Andy Lipkis, TreePeople is a nonprofit organization devoted to saving our ecosystem through education and tree planting. Trees process smog, produce oxygen, provide food, reduce the effects of drought, help retain moisture in the atmosphere, and are valuable for many other reasons.

TreePeople has been educating the public and planting trees for more than thirty-five years. Besides teaching people to plant and care for trees, TreePeople shows them many ways in which they can live more ecologically. Many of these methods are demonstrated at their mountaintop facility in the Santa Monica Mountains, which is still close to the hubbub of the big city.

One of their methods regarding how to live appropriately in the desert of southern California is to collect rain.

Adjacent to the TreePeople Center for Community Forestry is an underground concrete cistern that can hold 216,000 gallons of water. The idea that buildings can and should collect rain has helped determine the design of the conference center. Water collected from the roof, as well as from other parts of the property, flows directly into the cistern. The total catchment area is about two acres. Of course, a cistern of this size is more involved and costly than the average homeowner would need, but it shows what is possible, especially if planned into the construction of new buildings in deserts and drought areas.

According to David O'Donnell, an associate with the organization's Natural Urban Systems Group, "Fifteen inches of rain (our annual average) falling on a two-acre catchment would amount to roughly 800,000 gallons of water. We have no way of measuring actual inflow to the cistern, however, and we're not tracking our use of the stored water. So we don't know how much room might be available when it rains. I will venture a guess that we might capture between 40 and 60 percent of the total, depending on how the many variables interact." In theory, they could therefore fill the cistern twice each season.

A casual visitor does not see the underground cistern or any indication that rain is collected. A more perceptive visitor will see the uniquely sloped roof that can bring all the rain to a point, and they will notice what appears to be a large round sandbox for children directly where the runoff

Internal concrete rods support the large size of the cistern catchment system.

Continuing construction on the 216,000-gallon underground cistern.

from the roof might flow. The sand makes up the first layer of a filter that cleans the roof runoff before it enters the cistern. A layer or two of geotextile at the bottom of the filter finishes the job.

The filter housing is also a concrete cylinder, but it is much smaller than the cistern. It sits outside the circumference of the underground cistern.

When TreePeople needs to use the stored water, they simply pump it out of the cistern. It is then used for general landscape irrigation, including trees. The current construction project includes plans to build a watershed education garden and a new seedling nursery. The garden's water features will help TreePeople educators teach school children and park visitors about the problems and possibilities of urban watersheds. Trees

B.K. Bomar of TreePeople points toward the rain collection filter.

raised in the nursery will be planted in the local mountains to restore areas that were burned or otherwise impacted by human activity.

The cistern cost roughly $325,000, and the City of Los Angeles donated the excavation work, which would otherwise have been a significant additional expense. The cistern was paid for with donations given to help finance the construction of the TreePeople Center for Community Forestry.

I asked David O'Donnell how much such a rainwater collection system might add to the cost of a newly constructed home. "The cost per gallon of capacity is one way of thinking about this, but there are so many variables that it's difficult to come up with a meaningful estimate," he says. "Before we took down our old headquarters, we had a simple homemade

Bomar in front of the sand filter at the TreePeople Center for Community Forestry.

The conference center's roof is designed to facilitate rainwater collection.

system here that probably cost less than $200. I know of systems installed by serious do-it-yourselfers for a couple thousand dollars or less; more elaborate systems where everything is contracted out would probably run between five and ten thousand. If you built a system today, your cost per gallon of capacity would probably be between $1 and $3. Andy Lipkis likes to say that this cost could be as low as 50 cents if simple plans were available and modular units and accessories could be purchased at places like Home Depot."

So is it really possible to collect enough rainwater to make these kinds of systems worthwhile? Consider this: even if you collect *some* of your annual water this way, you will become a small part of the ecologic solution. So what if you can't collect all of your water needs from the rain? Start with what you can and grow from there.

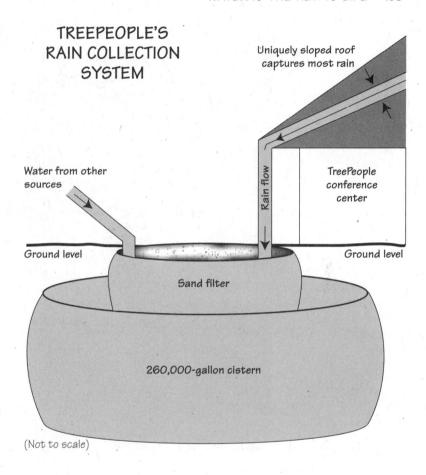

TREEPEOPLE'S
RAIN COLLECTION
SYSTEM

Uniquely sloped roof
captures most rain

Water from other
sources

Rain flow

TreePeople
conference
center

Ground level

Ground level

Sand filter

260,000-gallon cistern

(Not to scale)

Decades ago, I purchased new trash cans from a garden supply store in order to start collecting rainwater. I simply put the trash cans under the eaves where water collected, and I was easily able to fill five 30-gallon trash cans during each rain storm. (I put the lids on the cans as soon as they were full so mosquitoes would not breed.) That means I collected 150 gallons of water without even trying. I used most of the water I collected for the garden, fruit trees, and animals, and some I used for coffee.

The technology for capturing rain varies from culture to culture, depending on available materials, local rainfall patterns, local geology, presence of other water sources, and so on.

Trash cans are used to collect rain. They are situated at the edge of the roof overhang and covered when full or when the rain stops.

A portable and simple rain-collecting method consists of a large plastic sheet measuring about 4 by 8 feet, a few clothes pins, and a few 5-gallon jugs. After at least a half hour of heavy rain (to clean the air), you're ready to begin collecting rain.

Attach the plastic sheet to bushes so that it is somewhat stretched out and secure one corner so it forms a point. Place your water jugs under this flow of water; in a short period of time, the jugs will be full. A funnel, made by cutting off the top third of a 1-gallon jug, can also be helpful. A clean piece of cotton can be placed in the funnel to filter out small debris.

An easy way to collect small amounts of rainwater is to place a gallon container directly under the flow of rainwater from the roof. A large funnel is placed in the gallon container, and two sheets of at least 100-count cotton fabric are secured over the funnel as the filter.

If you're simply interested in seeing what you can collect, set out any sturdy buckets, barrels, or trash cans where water will flow into them, such as under your roof's valleys or under the downspouts of your house's gutters. But again, whatever you do, be sure to put tight-fitting lids on the containers when full. If you don't, you'll end up breeding mosquitoes that will irritate the entire neighborhood all summer.

The simplest method of collecting rain begins with placing various clean plastic containers around the house where water will flow into them. I don't currently have any rain gutters, so I place my containers under the roof valleys where the heaviest runoff occurs. When the containers are full, I cover them. About a day later, I clean out as many glass quart containers as necessary (these are recycled juice containers) and put a small funnel covered with a thick cotton filter on each container. I then siphon the water out of the rain collector containers (usually 5-gallon buckets) into smaller quart glass bottles. I then seal and store these quart containers in the kitchen to use for my coffee. I believe that the collected rainwater actually makes far better coffee than the water that comes from the tap.

FEASIBILITY OF COLLECTING RAINWATER

The performance of rainwater collection systems over a forty-year period at thirteen California locations was detailed in *Feasibility of Rainwater Collection Systems in California* by David Jenkins and Frank Pearson. They observed that, quite consistently, 88 percent of the annual California rain falls in the November-to-March wet season. The rain during this wet season is fairly well distributed, whereas the scant summer rain is highly variable with no observable pattern of distribution.

The authors of this study pointed out that rainwater collection is certainly possible at most homes, but it may not be cost-competitive with piped water due to the cost of storage tanks.

Relying on the rain as your main source of water is possible if you've properly calculated your water needs and have adequate storage tanks. Of course, the weather must also be cooperative for you to achieve a goal of rainwater self-sufficiency. I've never attempted to rely entirely on rainwater. I've rarely collected less than 30 gallons in a single storm, and on occasion, I've collected as much as 400 gallons of rainwater in a single downpour. That's water that I can use without relying on the piped water that comes to me from afar.

In some tests in urban areas, the rainwater contained lead concentrations equal or greater to the limit recommended for drinking water. This was primarily in the northeastern United States. Microbiological contamination of rainwater was found to be primarily from bird droppings on urban roofs. For these reasons, Jenkins and Pearson recommend that rain collected in urban areas not be consumed but instead used for washing or gardening.

We use rainwater primarily for the garden, fruit trees, and chickens. If I plan to use the rain for drinking, I first clean the containers well before putting them outside. I'll also cover the opening of the collection container with a sheet of cotton to filter out particles that may wash off the roof. If I forget to add the cotton filter, I'll wait a few hours after the rain stops to let particulates settle, and then siphon the rain out of the bucket into a clean jar. I may also run the water through a filter, such as the type that is sold at backpacking stores.

Due to the general alarm regarding acid rain, I test the pH level of any water that I intend to drink with a strip of litmus paper; litmus paper can be purchased at any chemical-supply store and at some hobby shops. Where we live in the hilly section of Los Angeles County, the rainwater we've collected has almost always been neutral. (Keep in mind that we never start collecting rain until after at least thirty minutes of a good downpour.)

HOW MUCH RAIN CAN I ACTUALLY COLLECT?

If you want to calculate the maximum amount of water that you can actually collect from rain, do the math. Begin by measuring the perimeter of your house (not your roof). Most roofs are slanted, and if you measure the perimeter of your roof, it will be larger than the house perimeter. The rain is falling more or less vertically, so you need to use the perimeter of the house as your figure. For this example, we'll say the house perimeter is 40 by 40 feet for a total of 1,600 square feet.

Next, find out the average rainfall in your area. In my area, the average is 15 inches, or 1.25 feet. If you don't know how much rain you get where you live, buy a rain gauge and secure it in an open area of the yard, away from trees and building overhangs. Rain gauges are easy to make yourself, but commercial models are inexpensive and have well-defined increments of measurement.

To calculate the possible volume of rain you can collect from your roof, measure the total square feet by the average rainfall in feet by 7.48 $(1,600 \times 1.25 \times 7.48)$. The total for our example is 14,960 gallons of rain water! That's a lot of water, but can you really capture it all? This depends on the configuration of the roof, but you most likely will not be able to capture all of the possible rain. If you have some sort of automatic system or wait thirty minutes after a heavy rain has begun to start collecting the rainwater, you will lose some of the potential water. Even if you have rain gutters and can actually capture most of the rain that falls on your roof, you should still deduct 5 to 10 percent of the above figure. In my case, my potential is about 14,960 minus 1,496 gallons (10 percent), which means if I am doing everything right and in a timely manner, I should be able to harvest 13,464 gallons of rainwater a year, give or take a few gallons.

A LAST WORD ON WATER

Recycling

Now that you've collected and used your rainwater, it would be a shame for it all to just go down the drain. It is actually quite easy in most situations to recycle some of your used household water back to your yard. In this case we're talking here about "gray water"—pretty much all the household water except that from the toilet.

Water from the kitchen sink may contain food scraps, which is good to use as a fertilizer. When you're done washing the dishes, simply carry the dish pan out into the yard and water a fruit tree or other plants. Obviously, if you intend to recycle your used water into your yard, you need to purchase detergents that contain few if any dyes or other additives that might be harmful to your plants.

Water from the bathtub and bathroom sink can be diverted under the house, assuming your situation is such that you can rely on gravity for the

Two different rain collectors are set up in an open area away from trees and buildings.

water to flow from the bathroom to the garden or yard. This requires going under your house, disconnecting the drain lines that flow from the bathtub and kitchen, and connecting new drain pipes that flow into your garden or yard. If you cannot rely on gravity, a more complicated system involving a small pump and possibly some holding tanks will need to be constructed. With some very basic plumbing skills, this is easy to accomplish, and you need only purchase the pipes and various connectors.

The cost will be higher, of course, if you need to hire a plumber. Talk to a few plumbers until you find one who understands what you are doing and why you are doing it. Simply replumbing your drain lines so the water flows directly into your yard will not meet the building codes in most cases. Since it can cost up to $10,000 to install a "city-approved" system that includes underground tanks, leach lines, permits, and more in order to recycle household water, most homeowners will not take that course of action.

It is also possible to fill 1-gallon plastic jugs with your bath or shower water and use them to manually flush your toilet. Pouring 1 to 2 gallons of water at once into a toilet bowl will cause it to flush. This is an ideal way to reuse water that might otherwise go down the drain.

Washing machines use a lot of water, even if you have an efficient low-water-use washing machine. In most cases, it is an easy matter to disconnect the drain pipe from the sewer line; they are simply connected with a clamp that requires only a screwdriver to remove. There are many ways in which to recycle your wash water. One way is to attach another hose to the washing machine's drain pipe and move the end of the hose to the garden. This needs to be planned so that gravity works in your favor, and the water can flow level or downhill to the garden.

When you become aware of each precious resource that you use, you will develop the desire to use these resources wisely and recycle where possible.

In a world with an ever-growing population, recycling our water helps us to be better stewards of the resources that flow through us. It makes good moral and ethical sense to recycle gray water, and it is ecologically sound to return your gray water to the soil rather than pump it away to the ocean or cesspool. It also makes economic sense to recycle gray water because you are using water at least twice that you paid for once.

We must also consider the consequences of wasting water and other resources. Clean, safe water is not limitless, and if we continue to disregard this fact, we will find ourselves in a world in which water needs to be rationed. The government spends little time on such issues, and society in general has only just begun to examine the long-term personal and national consequences of wasteful behavior. As with most considerations regarding natural resources, you'll need to find the system that works best for you and your family.

7

TOILET ALTERNATIVES

Toilets consume approximately 50 percent of the water coming into the average urban household. The various localized droughts from the 1970s led to the creation of toilets that use about a gallon and a half of water per flush, 70 percent less than the previous standard of five gallons per flush.

But is even that much water usage absolutely necessary to dispose of human waste? Perhaps some of our grandparents remember when out-houses were common in the United States. Most don't bring up great praises for the water savings, but instead speak of late night visits to a cold, often black widow–infested, smelly room. Certainly the outhouse concept is one that can be improved upon.

In the event of an emergency, you can always do as many campers do—dig a hole in a private spot, do your business, and cover the hole. If that solution seems less than ideal, there are several alternatives. What you do for a toilet in a post-disaster setting is almost entirely determined by how you planned in advance for dealing with a basic human activity that occurs several times a day.

I read about a family who decided to do a "survival test" to see how they would handle things if a major earthquake severed all utility lines and truck routes to their urban home. They turned off their water, gas, and electricity and only used the food, water, candles, and other miscellaneous resources they had stored in the home. They called off their test after a few days, however, when their emergency toilet ceased working properly. One wonders why they stopped their test just when it was becoming real. After all, when a crisis is suddenly upon us, we have no time for buying an alternative toilet—we just use whatever is available.

Human excrement is possibly one of the most overlooked areas in personal disaster planning. In our sophisticated modern society, we use the toilet, flush, and forget about it. Properly composted human excrement, however, can be a valuable source of fertilizer and even burnable gas, as the Chinese have proven.

According to Kou Jianping, director of the Energy and Zoology division of the Ministry of Agriculture, as of 2006, China had built biogas pits (pits into which fertilizers are placed and methane gas is produced) for 21.75 million households in rural areas and provided more than 5,200 large and midsize biogas projects based around livestock and poultry farms.

EARTHQUAKE TEST

As an experiment in human waste disposal, I once exclusively used a simple bucket toilet in my Los Angeles home for a period of three months. The test's purpose was to ascertain the practicality of such a toilet after an earthquake. When the bucket was nearly full, I emptied it into a trench in the outer yard, which I then layered with straw, earthworms, and worm castings. I eventually planted tomatoes in the trench.

The simple bucket was not difficult to set up or to use. We had to set up a rotation system for the three members of the household, however, so that each person took his or her turn in emptying the bucket, as no one was enthusiastic about this task.

Another challenge was to test various methods of combating the "outhouse odor" that many would find offensive. We tried some blue powder that came with the RV toilet, which worked okay. We also tried wood ash, and this too was acceptable. We didn't want to rely on a product provided by the manufacturer because in a "survival situation," when we actually would need to use this toilet, we'd probably not be able to readily get more of the blue powder. After trying many methods, we discovered that adding lemon juice and/or baking soda into the toilet after each use seemed to be the best solution to combat the odor.

Such a simple system could be done in the aftermath of an emergency when your sewer drain is broken, and as long as the participants emptied the bucket regularly and covered the hole where the contents were buried, this would be somewhat convenient as well as hygienic.

You could also use such a system as this on a more or less permanent basis if you were in the backwoods, too far from sewer lines and utilities; constructing an outbuilding (as people did for centuries), however, is a much more permanent fixture for a toilet.

THE WORM FARM

I conducted another test outdoors in a private, secluded part of the yard. I set up a hospital seat potty, and instead of the usual pot under the seat, I placed a large wooden box on the ground underneath. I placed a layer of earthworms, worm castings, and some partially decomposed straw inside the box. After each use of the toilet, I added another layer of earthworms and worm castings. The system was amazingly simple, odor-free, and fly-free. The real key to the success was the addition of the earthworms. The earthworms (I used red worms) are rapid reproducers, and they continually burrow and digest organic matter, breaking it down into a nitrogen-rich plant food. After each box became full, I simply put it to the side and let the worms process the contents. I would then place another empty box under the chair.

The worm farm idea came to me when I was observing a similar box I had established under my rabbit coop. The regular rabbit droppings and urine, which dropped through the screen bottom of their cage into the worm farm below, caused the earthworms to rapidly proliferate. With the worms processing the rabbit droppings, there was also a conspicuous absence of flies around the rabbits.

I was also motivated to pursue this project for another reason. Anyone who is concerned about the huge water—and potentially valuable fertilizer—waste in modern toilets has probably investigated commercial composting toilets. But even the cheapest of such toilets is nearly $1,000. I therefore attempted to find an easier, cheaper method that would still conform to all standards of health, cleanliness, and ease of operation.

A toilet such as this would save vast amounts of water and could be economically viable if set up properly. In wilderness areas such as national parks and remote cabins, a worm farm toilet makes far more sense than an outhouse method, in which the contents are considered waste matter at best and a health hazard at worst.

Kevin Sutherland shows a hospital porta-potty, which can be used as a toilet in emergencies. It can also be used as the basis for the worm farm .

Nonflush Composting Toilet

Christopher Reamer has also experimented with nonflush composting toilets. The easiest method, he says, is to simply use a bucket for your toilet, add some earthworms to the bucket when it's full, and set it aside for a while before dumping it out.

The system he built at his place in Malibu began with a commercially designed composting toilet that had been abandoned because it didn't work well. It housed a hand-powered mixing device designed to mix the waste with a prepurchased compost mixture. Enzymes were then added to speed up the decomposition. The finished product fell on a tray that could be emptied. The previous owner complained that the waste did not decompose fast enough in relation to how often it had to be emptied.

Reamer removed the internal parts and cut a space that would allow a 5-gallon bucket to fit inside. The waste then fell directly into a bucket, and a scoop of soil or mulch was added after each use. When the bucket was full, red worms (raised in a separate food-scrap compost pit) were added. The contents were then wetted slightly, capped, and left to sit for several weeks before being dumped selectively in the garden or orchard.

"We had a rotation of several buckets, all numbered, all in different stages of decomposition," says Reamer. "The opening of the first bucket surprised us with a forest of tomato sprouts, many more worms than were originally added, and no disagreeable odor whatsoever. Because we thought urine would perhaps interfere with the composting process, either by being caustic to the worms or by making the mixture too wet, we made a separate urinal that consisted of a two-foot-deep pit filled with gravel. Water from a hose was added after each use. This system drained well and never had any bad smell. A small house enclosed the toilet, the urinal, and a hose shower, all built from old pallets and other scrap materials."

Reamer designed the system this way because it was simple, needed little space, and used materials that were readily available and inexpensive. He added that the entire setup "can be put together, moved around, and taken down at the drop of a hat—like when our neighbors call the health department." This reminds us that "living green" doesn't always sit well with city hall.

One should always find out the pertinent law that pertains to any of your self-reliance projects. But keep in mind that urban planners and lawmakers are thinking about the lowest common denominator, *not* the fully awake, conscientious, self-reliant–striving person. For this reason, I recommend that you always get to know your local laws and especially your local leaders, lawmakers, and law enforcers, since it is *people* who must interpret and enforce the laws. It is still sometimes wise to "keep a low profile" about any of your projects that others in your community may not find acceptable.

Reamer used 5-gallon buckets because they are a size and weight that most people can move around when full of compost. You're constantly raising worms with this system, which are good in the orchard and garden. Such a toilet system uses a bare minimum of water, wholly unlike the conventional flush toilet in every home in America.

According to Reamer, "Separating the urine was an inconvenient part of our system. Perhaps a method could be devised where the urine could drain from the bucket in some way. I once worked at an organic farm in

Self-reliant experimenter Christopher Reamer next to a lean-to in which he spent three nights.

Maryland that had an interesting system consisting of a normal water flush toilet, which emptied into an old boat hull, a small canoe size. The hull was buried next to the house. Red worms and food scraps were added through an access panel. A pipe with a filter led out of the hull down a hill into a forest. This worked great for a while with virtually no maintenance, but when that filter finally plugged, the whole thing had to be shoveled out, by me."

Reamer also worked at a farm in Florida that had a dry-type composting toilet with separate holes in the bowl for urine and solids. Sawdust was added after each use. This system worked well except that the collection container was a big trash can, which was very difficult to move when full.

COMPOST TOILETS

Compost toilets can now be seen in most "green" catalogs depicting all the products that can make our lives more ecological. But how many of your friends actually use a compost toilet? Keep in mind that with a compost toilet in the bathroom, nothing is flushed away. No water is wasted, and no waste is sent to the nearest ocean or lake or wherever your sewers flow. Not all compost toilets are created equal, however. Some very large models are situated under the house so that both toilet and kitchen wastes will enter into a large holding area and decompose by way of their own heat. You can then remove the composted material and use it for fruit trees and nonroot crops.

Some smaller compost toilets use electricity for some heat or for a fan to help dry out the material entering the toilet. Some have a tank within the tank. In this design, the inner tank collects the solids, and it can be turned to speed up decomposition. Most manufacturers of these toilets have Web sites where you can examine the various possibilities. The choice you make will depend on your budget, the size of your household (how much material will be entering the toilet), and where you happen to live.

Compost toilets are not legal in most large urban areas. Don't expect your building and safety division to greet you warmly with open arms when you tell them how happy you are to "go green" with your compost toilet. This is one of the many areas in which one hand of local government doesn't know what the other hand is doing. The mayor expounds on

A Sun-Mar compost toilet.

Sun-Mars work by way of an inner chamber.

the values of "going green" by saving water and reducing resource uses, and then the legalistic folks at the codes enforcement division will fine you and tell you that such things as gray-water systems and compost toilets are not allowed.

Before purchasing an alternative system, get to know your local rules and regulations about any systems you want to try. If you then decide to have a compost toilet, do everything possible to maintain it as a model of ecological living. If you have such a toilet and let it become an eyesore, smell, attract flies, or you don't dispose of the contents hygienically, when you are exposed you will become an example of why such devices should continue to be outlawed.

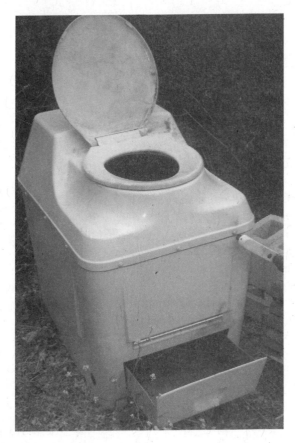

A Sun-Mar's clean-out drawer.

COMPACT SUN-MAR.

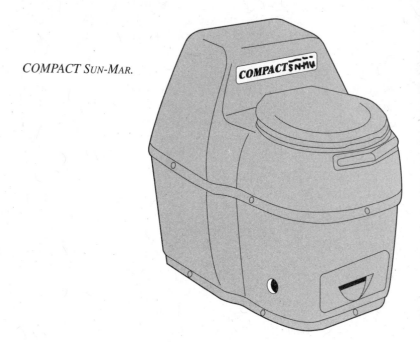

Clivus Multram Toilet

The Clivus Multrum toilet is often referred to as the Cadillac of compost toilets. The original Clivus Multrum composter was developed in 1939 by Swedish engineer Rikard Lindstrom. The name Clivus Multrum means "sloping chamber" in Swedish. The original Clivus used a single-chamber, sloped-bottom design and was constructed of concrete. The Clivus Multrum system was patented in 1962, and in 1964 the first commercial model was constructed out of fiberglass. In 1973, Clivus Multrum, Inc. was founded in Massachusetts under a license from Lindstrom. Clivus Multrum initially marketed its composting toilet and gray-water irrigation systems to homeowners.

The distinct sloping chamber remains a design feature of Clivus composters. Together with the custom-designed Clivus gray-water system, these technologies represent a complete on-site system for capturing and recycling nutrients.

In the mid 1970s, I met Martha Riley, who designed her Los Angeles home around her Clivus Multrum system. We knew Riley through her work as a piano tuner. She was an early outspoken ambassador for the virtues of a compost toilet and ecological living, back when the popular notion was that you were some sort of "nut" for being interested in such matters. Such is not the case today, but I was unfortunately unable to locate Martha when this book was being written.

Through the Clivus company, I learned that the Center for Urban Agriculture at Fairview Gardens in Goleta, California, uses one of the Clivus Multrum toilets. Fairview Gardens and the Center for Urban Agriculture is a nonprofit entity promoting organic and sustainable food production to the local community. The center is located in a semi-arid coastal zone along the Pacific where waste is typically flushed down a toilet, using at least two to three gallons of water to flush. The waste then goes through the sewer system to a waste disposal site where it is further treated with water to clean it, only to have it pumped out into the ocean to potentially contaminate the beaches.

I had the opportunity to speak with Matthew Logan about the decision to purchase a Clivus system. He explained that when they had planned to install a composting toilet many years earlier, his boss at the time learned about the Clivus through his research and discussions with other people in the area. They had previously used only portable restrooms rented from a local company.

The Clivus company offered a discount on the unit after learning that the Center for Urban Agriculture was a nonprofit organization and that many visitors to Fairview Gardens would learn about the toilet. The Fairview Gardens toilet is housed in a 300-square-foot building (called the bathhouse) that contains the toilet with the composting unit beneath the building, along with two shower rooms where the water is used to irrigate their avocado orchard. The center paid for the bathhouse with a grant through a local foundation, their own operating account, and with some money from donations. They hired someone to do the installation.

Compared with a conventional flush toilet, Logan described the use of the Clivus Multrum as "very easy." He then went on to say that a few problems exist. The panel in the composting unit that one opens to rake

Fairview Gardens' bathhouse facility shown from the outside. The facility consists of (on the far left) the composting restroom and (on the right) two shower units that are connected to a gray-water system that flow out to an avocado orchard.

The inside of the composting restroom.

The actual composting unit. It can contain up to two years of solid waste, which needs to be raked on a weekly or every-two-weeks basis through the upper opening. The liquid waste (below) needs to be removed every five to six weeks, depending on usage.

out the solid waste has too small of an opening, and when one rakes, it is sometimes very difficult to do a thorough job. The liquid waste pump is continually breaking down and the location of the pump itself may need to be redesigned." He nevertheless says that the toilet is very easy to clean, and it usually takes him about thirty minutes every two weeks to maintain it.

Logan explains that there are no special precautions to use the unit except to post signs about what can't be thrown into the toilet. When cleaning, one must wear a mask over the nose as well as plastic gloves. He adds that most guests have been extremely impressed with the unit and the fact that it does not take much to maintain it.

The Fairview Gardens composting toilet uses a very minimal amount of water, and the waste can be used as fertilizer on ornamental plants to enrich the soil. This is just one way in which the folks at Fairview Gardens represent a part of the solution to the problems facing all of us.

CLIVUS MULTRUM
ORGANIC WASTE TREATMENT SYSTEM

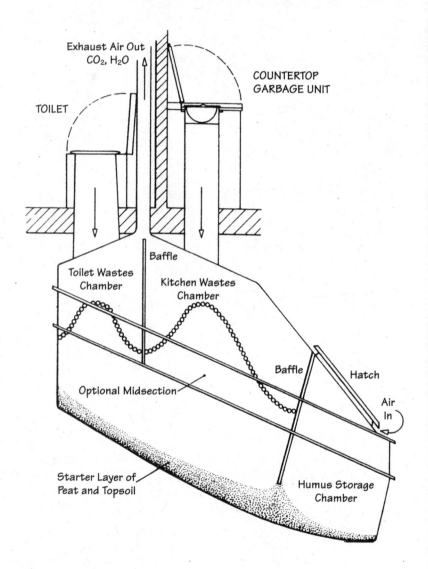

Exhaust Air Out
CO_2, H_2O

COUNTERTOP
GARBAGE UNIT

TOILET

Baffle

Toilet Wastes
Chamber

Kitchen Wastes
Chamber

Baffle

Hatch

Optional Midsection

Air
In

Starter Layer of
Peat and Topsoil

Humus Storage
Chamber

OUTHOUSES

Outhourses are still used in some areas such as remote campsites and rural areas. Whether they are old-fashioned with a moon over the door or all-plastic modern fixtures, outhouses can help us deal with a daily human biological necessity. Outhouses are viable in the aftermath of an emergency or in rural areas where it is either impractical to connect to sewer lines or too costly to build a septic system.

The main consideration in such structures is how to isolate the human waste until it can be composted or otherwise removed. One wants privacy, of course, and an environment free of flies and foul odors. Water supplies cannot be affected, so permanent outhouses must be located in suitable areas.

A portable outhouse.

Where possible, one can add red worms to the holding tank of the outhouse. These will breed rapidly and help reduce odors, assuming the liquid content and the temperature are not too high. Adding straw and grass to the holding tank after each use also helps the decomposition process; adding baking soda and lemon juice will help to combat bad odors. Sometimes it may be necessary to have incense or sage available in the outhouse to burn when the odors are too strong.

Modern temporary outhouses are cleaned out with a huge pump, which is then trucked away to a dump. If this is not an option, you will need to get a long-handled shovel and clean it out manually. All the contents should be buried in a prepared pit at least three feet deep. To help the decomposition process, add lots of red worms to the pit before covering it over. The outhouse should then be thoroughly scrubbed and rinsed out so the cycle can begin again.

BACKYARD METHANE DIGESTERS

We've discussed alternative toilets from the perspective of saving water and producing a usable fertilizer. These methods are worth considering in the aftermath of an emergency and in situations where you live far from the sewer lines, or when a septic tank is out of your budget.

Another consideration is that when fecal material, wood chips, and green plants decompose, methane gas is produced. Many people have experimented with ways to capture this methane gas and use it as a fuel.

Depending on your situation, a methane digester may or may not be practical. If you have the space to build and operate one, and if you have a regular supply of animal manure, a backyard methane digester may be a very practical way to produce some of your own fuel. Biogas is useful for running not only the stove, but also a refrigerator, lights, and even small motors.

Principles

Biogas is produced naturally whenever organic material is decomposed in the absence of oxygen. Plant matter in stagnant swamp water decays and gas is produced. This gas is sometimes ignited by static electricity or electrical storms, creating glowing fog or even fire.

If you create a small-scale swamp, you will have a methane digester. Your "swamp" can be inside any airtight container (wood, metal, plastic, cement, brick, and so on) into which you introduce organic matter (animal manures, grass clippings, certain leaves, vegetable scraps that readily decompose, and so on) in an oxygen-free environment.

To maximize the efficiency of this natural process, however, one must pay attention to the following factors:

1. *The pH of the material entering the methane digester.* A pH of 7.5 to 8.5 is best.
2. *The temperature.* Methane-producing bacteria thrive between 85 and 105 degrees. Below that range the bacteria won't produce gas, and above it they'll die.
3. *The solid to liquid ratio.* 6:1 is best, but remember that most fresh manures may be as much as 75 percent liquid.
4. *Carbon to nitrogen ratio.* 30:1 is best.

The most critical factor is keeping the upper temperature below 105 degrees F. Researching methane digesters in more detail before constructing one will help you avoid a multitude of problems.

Construction Details

There are many ways to build a methane digester. Two basic types of backyard methane digesters are batch feeders and continuous feeders. A batch feeder is filled and sealed (in a 55-gallon drum, for example), and when it has produced all the gas possible, you simply empty the container and start over. A continuous feed digester is given fresh material on a regular basis, while an equal amount is removed.

The simplest methane digester is a 55-gallon drum batch feeder. Put 10 gallons of water into the drum, 5 gallons of liquefied manure (cow, chicken, or other type), and enough shredded dry leaves and grass clippings to fill the drum almost two-thirds full.

You will ideally have a drum whose entire head comes off and seals with a rubber ring. If not, you'll have to get all the material into the large hole on the top of the drum. You'd then seal the large hole with a screw-in plug and rubber gasket.

First, screw a ¾-inch pipe nipple into the smaller hole and attach a tee. One end of the tee is reduced, and a plastic hose that directs the gas into

A SIMPLE BATCH FEEDER

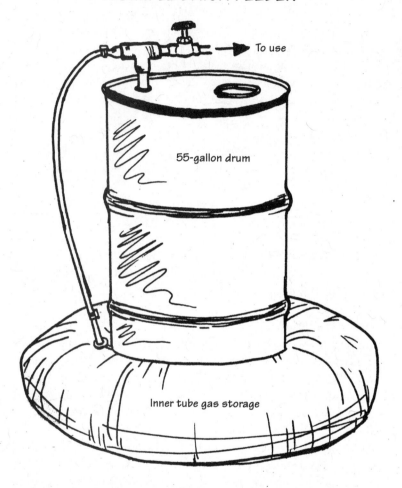

To use

55-gallon drum

Inner tube gas storage

the storage container (an old truck's inner tube is great) is attached. The other end of the tee is fitted with ¾-inch copper tubing, which leads to the stove or wherever the gas will be used.

With this system, you fill the drum two-thirds full with water and organic matter, seal it, and wait for the gas to develop. Depending on many variables, you might wait two days or two weeks. The drum system will eventually produce enough gas per day to burn for about thirty minutes. Three drums connected together should provide you with enough gas to cook at least three daily meals.

This isn't necessarily the best system, but it is simple, and no extensive building is involved. When the slurry (the swampy mush that the water and leaves turn into) in the drums has stopped producing gas, simply take off the piping, open the drum, and roll it over to empty into your garden.

The Kirkland White System

Gas shortages in the winter of 1976–77 inspired energy researcher Kirkland White's interest in home energy production. He researched how biogas is naturally produced from rotting material, and he began to experiment with ways to produce gas for his family's urban home in El Monte, California.

He built an inexpensive methane digester in his backyard that produced about an hour of gas each day. He built his continuous feed digester for about $150, using only simple hand tools and materials. He built it in his spare time over three weekends, and it produced about half of his family's cooking needs.

The digestion tank consisted of a 4 by 4–foot square box built of plywood and reinforced with two-by-fours. The inside was waterproofed with polyester resin. He built a tight-fitting lid but did not permanently attach it because of the occasional need to clean out the tank.

A 4-inch diameter pipe with a funnel was attached to the tank's lid for the introduction of new material. The pipe reached down below the water level so that no gas could escape. A 1/2-inch fitting was also installed on the lid so the gas could flow into a storage tank. An ingenious 4-inch diameter outlet valve—made from a PVC pipe and a piece of inner tube placed around the pipe—was built at the lowest point on the tank's side. When the inner tube was twisted, it effectively closed off the outlet valve.

White began by filling the tank with a mixture of cow manure and water to form a soupy slurry. He left the top off for two days to allow the initial carbon dioxide to be released. He then replaced the lid, and gas production began within two days.

His daily routine involved stirring the slurry with a 1/2-inch galvanized pipe stirring rod that went into the tank horizontally. He removed 5 gallons

APPROXIMATELY 400-GALLON
CONTINUOUS FEED DIGESTER TANK

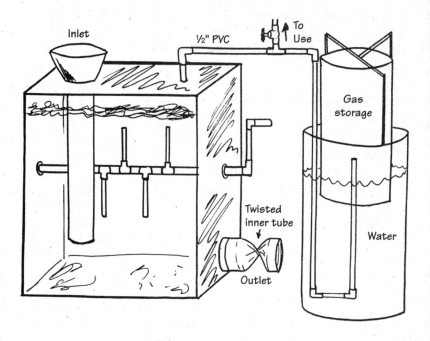

of old slurry every third day, then added 5 gallons of new material. He eventually used the slurry he'd removed in his garden. Although Kirkland did not devote much attention to pH, solid to liquid ratio, carbon to nitrogen ratio, and so on, he always made sure that the new material thoroughly mixed with water before introduction.

The storage tanks consisted of two 55-gallon drums, two-thirds filled with water, into which were placed inverted 30-gallon drums. From the digester, a ½-inch PVC line fed the biogas into the storage tank. The 30-gallon tanks would rise as they filled with gas; guide bars kept the drums in place. A valve at the storage tank could be opened or closed to allow the gas to go to his stove or into storage.

Biogas is a lower BTU gas than natural gas, so you'll need to enlarge the orifices on your appliances that use the biogas. This is usually a very simple procedure. Before you make any adjustment, however, check your appliance to determine whether it will burn the gas you're producing. Possibly no adjustment will be needed. If an adjustment is needed, make sure you do it correctly. If necessary, talk to an appliance expert who has experience in making such adjustments.

Kirkland White's system (or some variant) is recommended for those who want a simple, inexpensive-to-build and easy-to-maintain system to supply gas for their family's needs.

COMMUNITY METHANE DIGESTERS

From data I'd collected in 1982, I learned that China reportedly has one of the most aggressive methane programs in the world, with enough methane digesters throughout the country to serve about 35 million rural people. (The 2006 data suggest that the methane digesters now serve as many as 100 million people.)

Human manure is used in most of these digesters. The digesting pits render this "night soil" far safer for agricultural use than the former method of applying human manure from the outhouses directly to the fields. Two common digester designs are referred to as the Indian and the Chinese designs.

See the drawings on page 183 for a schematic comparison of each of these designs. In part, I learned about these from the *Biogas Newsletter*— a joint publication of the Gobar Gas Development Committee and the Department of Agriculture of Nepal—which I subscribed to in the late 1970s and early 1980s.

As you can see, each design has its pros and cons, and the selection would depend on your budget, skills, supply of building materials, availability and type of fertilizer, and fuel needs. The *Biogas Newsletter* states that both designs will give you excellent service if properly installed and operated. The newsletter also printed a comparison on the efficiency of each design in the winter of 1979, a summary of which follows.

Indian

The Indian gas plants are very satisfactory and serviceable. They are simple to build and maintain, and if intelligently operated, are virtually trouble-free. They are highly recommended, especially for beginners.

COMPARISON OF INDIAN AND CHINESE DIGESTER DESIGNS

	INDIAN	CHINESE
Purpose	Primary: gas production Secondary: fertilizer	Primary: fertilizer Secondary: gas production
Construction	Simple masonry pit; easy to build but hard to install where drum cannot be made or easily carried.	Closed underground masonry or concrete tank with adjacent effluent chamber; requires skill to render gas-tight; can be built anywhere.
Input	Virtually only cattle dung slurry. May serve as septic tank.	Mostly mixed organic matter (vegetable, dung, feces). Many of these plants are exclusively for night soil.
Output	Automatic gravity flow	By pump or bucket
Operation	Mostly flow fed. Almost never batch loaded. Virtually no attention beyond mixing and feeding slurry.	Can also work flow-fed with dung slurry. Generally batch loaded. Labor intensive for batch loading and emptying, and for removing effluent.
Gas collection	In floating drum: Height of float shows gas volume. Drum needs regular painting against corrosion.	No drum; gas sealed in digester: Gas volume and pressure shown by slurry height in outlet.
Gas pressure	Low: 70 to 100 mm water column. Steady, due to floating drum.	High: Up to 1,000 mm water column maximum. Constantly varying.
Cost	High because of metal drum and its fixture.	Lower cost because there's no metal.
Appearance	Presentable, neat	Neat, clean, unobtrusive

Chinese

The Chinese plants will also perform satisfactorily, but they require experienced builders. The high gas pressure in the digester poses the biggest problem if construction is not perfect (gas leaks or cracks in the cover and walls). This system is somewhat wasteful of gas; gas formed in side chambers is lost and excess pressure is reduced by releasing gas into the atmosphere. Relatively larger plants are therefore needed. The exhausted slurry and sludge of each batch makes richer and more abundant soil

INDIAN

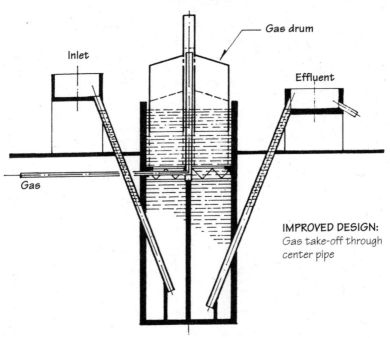

Inlet

Gas drum

Effluent

Gas

IMPROVED DESIGN:
Gas take-off through
center pipe

CHINESE

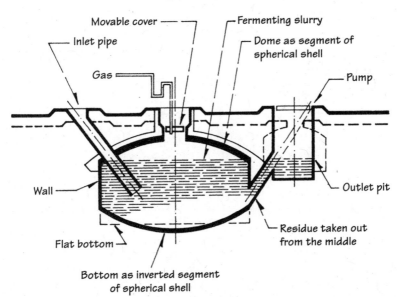

Movable cover

Fermenting slurry

Inlet pipe

Dome as segment of
spherical shell

Gas

Pump

Wall

Outlet pit

Flat bottom

Residue taken out
from the middle

Bottom as inverted segment
of spherical shell

COMMON ORGANIC MATERIALS AND
THEIR PRODUCTION FIGURES
Moisture Content, Nutrients, and Carbon/Nitrogen Ratios
Nutrients expressed in percent of dry weight

Type of organic materials	Lbs./day	% moisture	Nitrogen	Phosphorus	Potassium	C/N ratio
Human feces	0.45	73	6.0	4.2	1.8	8.0
Urine (dry)	0.14	94	17.0	3.7	3.7	0.8
Cow, dairy	72.0	80	1.7	1.1	0.56	25.0
Beef:						
Fed on alfalfa	90.0	80	2.6	—	—	16.0
Fed on grain and rice hull bedding		78	2.0	—	—	21.4
Horses, oxen, mules	60.0	75	2.3	1.3	1.4	25.0
Pigs	9.0	82	3.8	3.1	2.5	14.4
Sheeps, goats	3.3	68	3.8	1.9	1.3	20.1
Rabbits			1.7			
Turkey		75	4.2			8.3
Chickens, pigeons	0.35	56	6.3			5.3
Sawdust (raw)			0.11			511.0
Grass clippings		65	2.2			19.0
Straw oats			0.52			83.0
Leaves (ripe)		50	0.2			203.0
Blood			12.0			3.0
Flesh			5.1			
Kitchen scraps:						
Garbage		72	3.3			16.0
Fats		0	0			76.0
Rags		10	4.6			12.0
Dirt, household		3.2	0.5			41.0
Sugarcane trash			0.35			113.0
Wheat straw			0.33			124.0
Maize stalks and leaves			0.84			53.0

conditions than that of the Indian design. The digester, because it is totally underground, is better insulated against winter cold (if it is located in dry soil).

Remember the carbon/nitrogen ratio mentioned earlier? The chart on page 184 gives you an idea of the carbon/nitrogen ratio of various organic materials, as well as their percentage of nitrogen, phosphorus, and potassium. Les Auerbach drew upon several sources to create this chart, which was originally published in his booklet *A Homesite Power Unit: Methane Generator.*

Auerbach's booklet explains how to create a home gas production unit, based on items that you should be able to easily obtain in the United

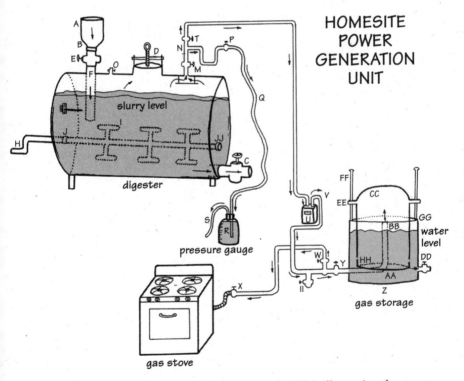

Schematic diagram of Homesite Power Generation Unit illustrating the components and assembly features, fully described in Les Auerbach's A Homesite Power Unit: Methane Generator.

States. The illustration shows his basic system. The picture is somewhat self-explanatory, where materials are added at A and enter the large decomposition tank. H is a mixing rod. C is a clean-out valve where you remove materials as you add new materials. The gas produced by this system is either fed to a storage container or to an appliance, such as a stove.

8

FOOD PRODUCTION
AND SELF-RELIANCE

Most beginning gardeners are concerned with what kind of plants they should grow or how they can keep insects from destroying their crop. Although these questions are certainly valid, I would rather approach the broader topics of how to grow food in an economically and ecologically sound manner. Every situation, and every yard, is different; what I think will or will not grow in someone's yard is irrelevant. If your goal is to become more self-reliant and produce some of your food and medicine in your backyard, then let's consider what you already have.

START FROM THE BEGINNING

You should first take inventory of what is already growing in your yard. Which plants are natives and which are introduced exotics? Is the yard carefully tended, or are these plants just growing wild? If you are not familiar with the plants in your yard, you can hire a botanist or gardener to tell you the names of the plants and their possible uses. Learn about the bushes, trees, ornamentals, vines, flowers, and weeds. You might already have useful plants in your yard that are surviving well with whatever care they are getting.

After you survey what is growing in your yard, you might find that you already have some food resources available. Knowledge is the key to opening this door. You might also determine, however, that some or many of the plants should be removed because they do not serve your self-reliance purposes. If you remove trees, cut them into fireplace-sized logs so you can burn them next winter. If you remove any bushes or shrubs, add them to your compost pile or put them through a chipper so they can continue to provide your yard with fertilizer. Before you begin any cutting, consider other uses of the plants you will be removing. Are there long branches that can be made into walking sticks or tool handles? Do some of the bushes contain sticks that might serve as trellises for your garden? Are there vines that could be constructed into baskets? In other words, learn to look at everything differently.

If you are like most urban and suburban homeowners, you have a front lawn that is simply "wasted space" in most cases. Front lawns are relics from a bygone era that most of us do not need. The maintenance of a lawn requires water, fuel, fertilizer, and lots of time, all for the sake of having a green lawn. In many urban areas, folks are foregoing front lawns in order to plant roses, herbs, cacti, and otherwise make the space more useful.

In what was formerly a lawn, edible nasturtiums now grow along with wildflowers.

Instead of a lawn, these folks opted for lavender and rosemary.

SO WHAT DO I GROW?

Entire libraries of books have explained in great detail everything you need to know about gardening. Sunset books are excellent, as are publications by Rodale Press, from their *Organic Gardening* magazine to their *Complete Book of Composting* and *Encyclopedia of Organic Gardening*. These and others are useful references that will provide you with a life-time of information. I also recommend that you read Masanobu Fukuoka's *The One-Straw Revolution* for a more philosophical guide.

I have read many exciting accounts from urban homesteaders who explain why they chose each and every variety of plant, and who even pro-vide maps for the ideal way to lay out a garden. Take such advice with a grain of salt; what works for one individual may or may not work for you.

You should therefore start by making a comprehensive list of what you and your family like to eat. You always have the opportunity to expand your garden as your food tastes expand. You might also consider plants that will provide you with medicine and other useful items (such as the silk floss tree, which provides a downy material for pillow stuffing). Also take into account fragrances you want in your yard, as well as those which may attract birds and other animals you'd like to welcome. Think of your yard or garden as a small biosphere that has the potential to provide many of your needs.

After taking all these factors into consideration, your resulting list will probably be long. Your next task will be to obtain a gardening guide for the area in which you live and ascertain which plants are most likely to do well in your area. If you live in Pennsylvania, delete bananas and papayas from your list, as they probably won't do well unless you intend to have a greenhouse. With the help of a gardening guide and advice from a local farmer or nursery worker, you should be able to whittle down your list to the plants that are known to do well in your area.

Once you have an idea of what you want to grow, you could simply purchase seeds and plants and start planting. If you are a bit more serious, however, you could draw a map of your yard to plan where to put every-thing—don't forget to sketch in the plants that are already there. Also keep in mind how the new trees, bushes, vegetables, and others will be affected by the sun (and shade), and how they'll affect (or be affected by) the prevailing winds, roof overhangs, walls, walkways, and so on.

If you intend to have vines, plant them along preexisting fences or walls that get sufficient sun. If you intend to plant trees, be sure to take into account the shade they'll cast underneath and how this might cut down on your vegetable crops. In general (for North America), you'll want your trees in the northernmost parts of your yard so they won't shade your vegetable garden.

Deciduous trees will lose their leaves in the winter, which will make a good mulch and ground cover if just left on your yard. Evergreen trees don't lose their leaves, so they will provide shade year-round. Be sure you know which trees are which before you plant them; avocados and citruses are evergreens, for example, whereas apples, plums, and apricots are all deciduous.

SOURCES OF SEEDS AND PLANTS

You could just order seeds from catalogs, or you could drive down to your neighborhood nursery and purchase all the plants you wish to have in your garden. There's nothing wrong with doing either of these things. Another option is to cultivate your own land so it can provide you with all the fertilizer and plants you need; this is one of the principles of permaculture.

First, look at all the seeds you routinely discard in your kitchen. If there were no catalogs from which to purchase seeds and no nearby stores or nurseries, you would use every one of those seeds for the next generation of your garden. We often overlook many of our common resources because we simply don't recognize what is right in front of us.

Seeds

Seeds from watermelon, cantaloupe, and all squashes (such as spaghetti squash and pumpkin) can be saved and planted. (You will think twice before buying any "seedless" watermelon.) These sprawling vines require a large amount of horizontal space to grow. Seeds from grapes and beans can also be planted. Both of these vining plants require vertical space to grow, so they should be planted next to a fence or trellis. Seeds from bell peppers and hot peppers can all be saved and grown in your garden.

Tomato seeds are easy to extract and can be immediately planted. They tend to be some of the easiest seeds to grow. Tomato plants grow under a broad variety of conditions and will produce quality fruits better than you get at any market.

Seeds from most fruits can be saved and grown. Citrus seeds, for example, will produce the same fruit as the parent about 80 percent of the time. I have sprouted hundreds of citrus seeds, although not all have survived. Apple trees can be grown from seeds, and each tree has the potential to produce a new variety of apples. One of my favorite apple trees was grown from an apple core that I put in my car's ash tray. Eventually, I cleaned out the ash tray with the old apple core into a flower pot. Imagine my surprise when an apple seed sprouted! It is now about 10 feet tall with delicious Gala-like fruit.

Seeds from all stone fruit can be planted. This includes all varieties of peach, plum, nectarine, cherry, apricot, and so on. I eat the fruit from several trees that I have grown from seeds. Avocado seeds can also be planted

You can harvest seeds from any tomato. Here, Timothy Snider shows the seeds of an heirloom tomato.

to produce a tree, although seedlings only produce fruit about 25 percent of the time, so grafting is usually required to ensure that your tree will produce fruit.

While you might think these are not the kinds of plants you want to grow in your garden, they are nevertheless foods you are already eating. Save and plant the seeds. If nothing else, plant them in pots so you can sell or barter the resulting plants with your neighbors.

Vegetative Growth

In addition to using seeds from your kitchen, you can also produce plants in your garden from "old" vegetables that have started to sprout. I routinely take all my potatoes that have begun to sprout and are too old to eat and bury them in suitable places in my garden. Since I end up planting periodically year-round, I always have potatoes in my garden. The gophers

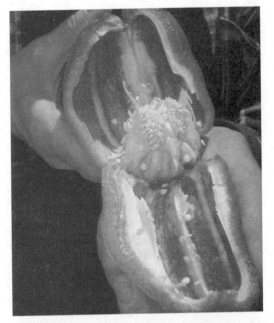

Red pepper seeds are easily harvested and grown.

Avocados grown from seed.

eat most of my potatoes, but I still plant enough so that I end up with a sufficient supply for boiled potatoes and potato salad.

You also don't need to discard sprouted garlic or onion. Just dig a small hole and plant them. You can then harvest a bulb later in the season or simply pick the greens.

Sometimes a head of celery gets too old and limp to eat, but it is actually continuing to grow from the center. I peel back the old stalks and plant the inner core of the celery in the ground. Although not all of these have grown, enough of them have to prove that it can be done. Some of my celery grown this way has gone to seed and produced new generations of celery.

You can also take carrot tops and plant them directly in the ground. Cut off the greens with about an inch or two of the carrot. Old radishes can also be planted, and although the next generation's roots will be too tough to eat, you will get a perennial crop of "radish greens" every spring for salads or cooked greens

Cuttings

I've said many times that your land can provide you with all the plants you need. It's important, however, to have a broad definition of "your land" that includes "your neighborhood." Individual, private, exclusive self-reliance is *not* what I'm talking about. Your neighbors are not your enemies, and the sooner you educate your neighbors to the practical viability of using their land, the better.

In just about every neighborhood, people have a lot of a few things, and rarely does one person have everything. Get to know your neighbors. If you don't already have a Neighborhood Watch organization, start one. If not a Neighborhood Watch, then find any reason for the neighbors to come together in some regular way. During these meetings, you can find out if anyone has plants they can share with others.

If someone has a fig tree, for example, each of the pruned cuttings can be planted to grow a new fig tree. Not all trees or vines are easily sprouted by cuttings, but many are. Some of the easiest cuttings to cultivate are figs, apples, pears, roses (remember rose hips and petals are edible), mulberry (make sure it is a fruiting variety), grape vines, and currant vines.

Maybe a neighbor grows a good variety of prickly pear cactus, which has delicious fall fruits and a year-round supply of green pads. You can simply take a pad of the cactus and plant it in your yard. It will take a few years of growth before it starts producing prolific pads and fruits.

Jerusalem artichokes are a variety of sunflower with edible tubers that are cooked like potatoes. Those who grow these plants may find that the tubers very soon take over much of the yard, and they are soon begging their neighbors to take some. The great thing about Jerusalem artichoke is that you can plant it once (plant one tuber per hole), and by the end of the season, each tuber grows into a large cluster of tubers. If your soil is good and you don't have an abundance of gophers, you'll have Jerusalem artichokes forever.

Start cultivating food crops at home. Get to know your neighbors and find out what resources they have available. You might be surprised at the relative abundance you already have once you begin to look at things differently.

FIGURING THINGS OUTS

When I was still living with my parents, we had no area at all to garden. It was unthinkable at that time to tear up a front lawn and use it for a garden—something I wouldn't hesitate to do today. Our next-door neighbor offered us the use of an empty yard between our houses. My mother—who grew up on a farm—sat up at night with me planning how to use that space for gardening. Most of what I learned about planting was learned by making mistakes.

I began by planting herbs, tomatoes, and corn, all neatly arranged in north-south lines with some pathways in between. I knew nothing about fertilizer or mulch or pest control. I just went out there and planted what I believed would make the best garden, and I watched the results.

The herbs—mints, fennel, oregano, lavendar, and others—took care of themselves. Herbs tend to be drought-tolerant and require very little time and effort. Tomatoes grew well, too, but I learned that they just grew and grew and would only begin to produce lots of tomatoes when I pinched back the stems so the branches would not grow as long. Yes, I got tomato worms, which I just picked off and tossed to the birds.

Growing corn was quite educational. It grew tall and the ears formed. As they got bigger, I noticed that they were infested with lots of ants, aphids, and earwigs. In horror, I would take the hose and wash all the bugs off, which worked to some extent because it was a small garden.

That first season's corn was a disaster, with bug-infested, half-developed ears; I had used some bug poison for the first and last time. I experimented with some of the natural pest repellants and made my own insecticide from a mixture of garlic and hot peppers, liquefied in a blender and sprayed on the plants. I even added a little Basic H to the mix. I had some good results, but I was still working with poor soil. In desperation, I studied all I could on natural pest control. After all, shouldn't farming and gardening be about life, not death? Can't nature take care of itself? Isn't there a way to find a balance so that the bugs keep the other bugs in check?

Build the Soil

Regardless of what you grow or where you live, the *health of the soil is the single most important factor* in producing plants that are drought-tolerant, bug-resistant, and able to survive in the greatest range of temperatures.

When I had only that small yard to garden, I would get boxes of old produce from the grocery store, dig some holes around the garden, and bury the old vegetables so they'd decompose and enrich the soil. I also went to the local cemetery and obtained bags of grass clippings. I began to layer the bare ground around the base of the plants with liberal amounts of grass clippings. This was a thick layer, not a thin sprinkling of clippings. The top layer would dry out a bit, but underneath it stayed moist, softened the soil, and provided an environment where earthworms and many other bugs thrived. With the layered grass clippings on the ground, I noticed that the herbs and vegetables thrived and grew well, and the bug infestation was at a minimum. I also didn't need to water as often. I continued to get as many bags of grass clippings as possible and mulched the soil. And I continued to bury old vegetables in the garden. I produced onions, tomatoes, Swiss chard, zucchinis, and lots of herbs. I decided to skip the corn.

A SIMPLE GARDEN

A few years later, I lived in a house in a hilly part of Los Angeles with an enclosed yard. I kept some ducks and grew many vegetables, including corn. I had tomatoes and peas and vegetables. I didn't bring grass clippings there, but I did maintain a compost pit where I produced my own fertilizer from kitchen and yard scraps. One day, I had a tree pruner dump a massive truckload of wood chips in my yard, and I used them to mulch every square inch of my garden. At night, I would put the hose in my corn patch and let it dribble out. The ducks would spend the evening there, and they loved to eat all the earwigs and whatever other bugs the water brought out.

The corn grew tall and strong. One day, my friend David Ashley and I stood in the corn patch eating raw corn. David had assumed that corn had to be cooked and was amazed at the sweetness of the raw corn. We stood there for fifteen minutes or so talking, and David was amazed that the experience of standing in my little duck-fertilized corn patch was like being in another world. It was like my own postage stamp–sized "field of dreams," my own Walden Pond. David talked about it for years afterward.

In this garden, I grew only nonhybrid varieties whose seeds I could harvest and replant. These were the vegetables also known as the heirloom varieties. At the time, I was not aware of how today's farmers are captive to the corporations that produce hybrid seeds, the widely touted miracle of modern farming. I was always disturbed about hybrids, whose seeds would not produce the same plant that they came from. Whenever possible, I would obtain and use the nonhybrid, or heirloom, seeds, and I would save some of the seed for the next season, just as small farmers and families have done for centuries.

Part of my garden was the famed three sisters of the Southwest—corn, squash, and beans, which David Ashley suggested I grow. Squash is planted and allowed to sprawl on the ground as a ground cover, keeping some moisture in the soil. Corn is planted throughout the area, and once the corn gets a foot or so tall, native beans are planted. The roots of the beans fix nitrogen, meaning that you are increasing the nitrogen content for your corn by growing the beans nearby. Corn also provides a trellis of sorts for the beans. This "three sisters" garden is a common theme in arid Southwestern gardens.

BUILDING AND UTILIZING COMPOST PITS

I have gardened and worked the soil since about age twelve, and I've learned that the most important thing to do to produce a bountiful garden is to improve the soil. Since every household produces kitchen scraps, and most yards produce grass clippings and various leaves, one of the very first steps in urban self-reliance is to set up a compost system so you can begin to produce your own compost from those items that you typically discard.

There are endless ways to obtain a composter. You can go to a garden supply store and simply buy one. Store-bought models are typically plastic devices that look like upside-down trash cans. They might be round or square, but there will always be a hatch at the top for adding material and a door on the bottom for removing the compost once it has become good soil.

Store-bought composters provide an easy way to compost organic materials in your own backyard.

On the farm in Ohio, my brother and I used an old raised garden bed—an approximately 3 by 5–foot area enclosed by boards—for our compost area. We collected vegetable scraps from the kitchen and put them into the area, and we kept a piece of plywood over the top to keep out mice and rats.

I have also taken old plastic trash cans, which have tight-fitting lids, and cut out the bottoms of the cans. I would replace the bottom with screen, then put the composter in the garden area. All kitchen scraps, leaves, and small branches from the garden would go into the composter. Any moisture went into the soil, and the screen and tight lid kept out mice and rats. Plus, once you get a lot of material into such a composter, it gets very hot and speeds up decomposition.

I have stacked old tires three to five high, placed a piece of carpeting over the top, and added vegetable scraps, leaves, and more to the center hole. Stacked tires also make for a hot composter with quick decomposition. If you properly locate such a composter, you can eventually take your shovel and just shovel finished compost from the bottom as you continue to add to the top opening. I have also simply covered the stack of tires when full and started another. I would go back to the first one after some passage of time and just knock the stack over so the good compost would spread in the garden. I have also planted tomatoes in a full tire stack.

I have made composters for large volumes of yard leaves and scraps by nailing four pallets together and using a fifth pallet for a lid, or just leaving it open. I have also made composters from a roll of chicken wire turned into a large tube, which I stood up in the yard or garden and began adding organic matter to it.

Because composting devices can be made from most materials, there is really no need to buy a commercially made device. You should, however, build something that is fitting to the materials you will be composting. You don't need anything too large if you'll only be dealing with kitchen scraps from one or two people. But if you also have a large yard with lots of leaves that you rake and a lawn that you cut, you'll want a larger composting system.

Consider the following when thinking about constructing a composter:

Location. Put the composter both where it is convenient, ideally near where you will use the compost. But also take sunlight into account—more sun will mean hotter compost, which means quicker decomposition.

You don't want your composter on a cement or brick surface but instead on the soil where liquids will just soak in.

Border. A composter contains vegetation so it will decompose on its own. The border can be wood, brick, chicken-wire, or an old trash can, as long as it defines the area where all the vegetation will be put. Just about anything can be used to contain and define your compost area.

Pests. The decomposition of vegetation carries with it strong odors and lots of insects and larvae that feed on the decomposition. Insects are therefore going to be a part of this process. The heat produced by decomposition will kill many of them, however, and some will retreat to the outer, cooler edges of the compost device. But you do not want to breed mice, rats, mosquitoes, yellow jackets, roaches, or any other undesirable creatures that might spread disease and otherwise make your life miserable. Put a screen on the bottom of your composter to keep creatures from burrowing into the bottom of your device. Some sort of a lid should also be used to cover the compost area; I have used pieces of plywood, old carpeting, and other boards to keep it "closed." Of course, most commercial composters are self-contained and will help you avoid these problems.

Remember, composting is the epitome of simplicity. Don't fret if things are not composting correctly. With a little effort, you can create high-quality compost faster. Check to make sure that the pile is moist and aerated enough to facilitate bacterial activity. Add brown (carbon-rich matter such as dry leaves, rotted hay, small sticks, or plant stems) and green (nitrogen-rich matter such as grass clippings or garden trimmings) for the more or less ideal carbon to nitrogen ratio of 20 or 25 to 1.

WORMS

Earthworms are a gardener's friend because they constantly eat bits of vegetation as they burrow through the soil and leave their nitrogen-rich castings everywhere. Do whatever you can to encourage earthworms in your garden.

My friend Jeff Philipps gardens at a community garden and produces a lot of his own produce. As he gardens, he regularly picks earthworms out of the soil and puts them into one area where they proliferate. He never went out and purchased earthworms but simply encouraged them to grow. Now he has earthworms all over in the rich soil of his garden.

One of the best things that Dolores and I ever did was to buy red worms—I believe we purchased them from a place that sold fishing supplies, so they were meant to be used as bait. In our new home, we created a square space about 4 by 5 feet large of railroad timbers. We simply put kitchen scraps directly into this area and covered them with soil after each use; we also put some of the floor rakings from the chicken coop into the compost pit. We added the red worms to the edge of the compost area, and they always gravitated to whatever new compost we added. If we added a lot of new material, the worms would retreat from the heat of the decomposition. We therefore always had to be careful to never add too much at one time.

This system was a combination worm farm–compost pit, and it was large enough so that the worms had space to move away from the heat. Red worms are often regarded as the ideal worm for most compost systems because they multiply rapidly, and they can tolerate the greatest range of temperature. There are other worms one can use—such as the large night crawlers anglers like—but most have very specific and narrow temperature ranges and other soil requirements. Red worms are not the largest, but they multiply amazingly fast and soon you'll see, as we did, that you have enough red worms to give bucketfuls to neighbors who also want to start compost systems.

One time when I cleaned out the chicken coop, I added a large amount of their nitrogen-rich manure to the worm farm–compost pit; a "large amount" was probably about two wheelbarrows full. Unfortunately, this all should have gone into a hot composter, for after the chicken manure was watered, it got so hot that it killed off most of the red worms. For weeks afterward, I had to carefully nurture the red worm population back to its previous levels by carefully monitoring what I added.

Every time a tree was planted or some new crop was added to the garden, I'd take several shovel scoops of the wormy compost and add it to the hole where the new tree or crop was planted. This wormy compost is perhaps the greatest unsung miracle that any gardener has ever used. This is a genuine benefit to the long-term life of the soil and garden, not the bogus "miracle" that many commercial products promise. I avoid all commercial additives and fertilizers.

MULCH

Mulch is anything you can simply lay on the ground without worrying about it attracting flies, rodents, or roaches. Mulch can be such things as grass clippings, wood chips, wood shavings, small pebbles, coffee grounds, and many others.

Mulch can do many things depending on the environment where you live and your specific needs. Probably the most important is that a mulch layer helps reduce water loss from the soil, especially in arid climates. Moisture is always evaporating out of the soil; this is how nature's water cycle works. Soil that is bare of vegetation—like in the desert—is not evaporating much because most of the moisture has already been lost. When you mulch the soil, you create a barrier to that water loss, which helps slow some of that evaporation. A moist layer of small living organisms begin to form just under the surface. This layer of life helps to retain some moisture and makes the soil more supportive of life.

Mulching also is used to do away with unwanted vegetation and promote those plants you wish to cultivate. This occurs because heavy mulch temporarily creates an environment where unwanted vegetation won't grow, and strategically placed mulch will benefit desirable plants.

As the lower layer of mulch decomposes, it becomes fertilizer. This is a slow fertilizer, because it takes some time for the successful breakdown of wood chips into soil by the mycelium of fungi and other factors. Slow is okay, though, for you should always be thinking about ways to improve the soil, and long-term thinking is always better than short-term thinking.

FERTILIZERS

Find a way to use ordinary discards to create your own fertilizer. Fertilizer, by definition, is anything that enriches the soil, so any kitchen scraps you toss into your composter can become fertilizer. Your old eggshells are therefore a form of fertilizer. They are 93 percent calcium carbonite, and calcium is an essential nutrient in plant cell manufacture and growth. Save your eggshells, crush them coarse or fine, and scatter them around the plants that need calcium.

Mulching currant vines.

A heavy layer of wood shavings can be used as mulch.

Save your old coffee grounds, which contain about 2 percent nitrogen, about one-third of 1 percent phosphoric acid, and less than 1 percent potash. Coffee grounds are particularly useful on those plants that we'd label as "acid food," such as blueberries, evergreens, roses, camelias, avocadoes, and certain fruit trees. I often add coffee grounds to my tomato plants and find that the tomatoes seem to be improved.

MANURES

In terms of manure choice, I have one simple rule of thumb: get whatever manure you can get *for free*. Horse manure is usually free for the taking wherever there is a horse stable. Horse manure is not the best quality manure, however, and it may have a strong odor for a few days and may even contain horsefly larvae. To offset this, I bring small amounts of horse manure into my garden at a time. I will also sometimes add fresh horse manure directly into my composter so it will lose the smell, and the heat will kill off fly larvae. I have seen many excellent gardens whose main fertilizer was horse manure. I am not a big fan of spending money if I can get something that is similar or the same without paying for it.

Anyone who has chickens would most likely let you rake out their chicken house and fill some large bags with the rakings. Chicken manure is good, but you rarely get just the manure. Rather, you are raking up decomposed straw, old food particles, soil, and manure. Still, this makes a good free fertilizer.

Rabbit droppings have been described as "nature's time-capsule" fertilizer. They do not smell, and they can actually just be tossed around under the plants that need them. There are probably more "rabbit farmers" in the city than we know about, since rabbits are quiet and take up very little space. For years I raised rabbits only for their ability to make top-quality compost. I have also used the manure from my pet pot-bellied pig, Otis, around newly planted trees and plants that I thought needed some nutrients. Amazingly, I always observed that the plants that were fed Otis manure showed a rapid improvement.

If you are interested in the nitrogen content of manures, there are many agricultural tables you can consult. You can learn the amount of nitrogen, phosphorus, potassium, and so on from both fresh and dried manure. When manure is dry, the nitrogen is more concentrated, so you will read a higher figure for dried versus fresh manure. I have noted that the figures from different sources are always a little bit different, probably due to variations in the animals' feed, different testing conditions, and other variables.

Based on a percentage of dry weight, for example, rabbit manure has about 1.7 percent nitrogen, horse manure has about 2 to 2.3 percent nitrogen, pig manure has about 3.8 percent nitrogen, and chicken manure contains from 4.5 to 6.3 percent nitrogen.

LIGHT

The light in your yard may change throughout the day and throughout the year. This can have a dramatic effect on your garden. Some plants will do best in direct sunlight for the longest time possible, while others tend to thrive in the shade and mixed light under trees.

Garden books, such as those by Sunset, explain the light requirements for all garden plants. Be sure to take this into account before you do your planting. Of course, in many cases, you only have one spot to garden so you'll just need to make the best of it.

LEARN THE WEEDS

Most so-called common weeds are edible and nutritious. To learn about these plants, take samples to a botanist at a college, or show the plant to a skilled plant expert at a nursery. Participate in plant walks so you can learn about the common wild plants that grow around your home and in your neighborhood. (It might be interesting to learn about exotic herbs that grow in the rain forest, but this information won't help you out after the next hurricane or earthquake, unless you actually live in a rain forest.) Learn what is local.

The best way to learn is through first-hand experience, seeing and trying the plants with someone who already knows what they are. Also, there are some good videos out there to help you along if you just can't go on a nature walk.

PEST CONTROL

Everyone wants to know how to keep bugs out of the garden. However, insects and various bugs are a part of nature; they are part of the process that continually turns organic matter into soil and part of nature's cycle of predator and prey. The goal of pest control in a natural context is not to create an unhealthful environment for the people who live there, but to create an environment where nature will find its own balance, where good bugs eat the bad bugs, and where healthy plants are more resistant to insects.

First, you must improve your soil. Insects primarily attack plants that are sick or deficient in some vital nutrient, so improving the soil renders your plants less susceptible to ravaging insects, as well as to the extremes of heat, cold, and drought.

Planting herbs next to your vegetable crops is believed to repel insects. *Rodale's All-New Encyclopedia of Organic Gardening* mentions many plants that are said to repel bugs from other garden plants, such as borage and basil around tomatoes to help deter tomato worms and other bugs. In general, try to mix your herbs throughout your garden to create the kind of garden you might see it in the wild. Rarely do you see neat tidy rows in nature, with clean and raked soil underneath.

You can also purchase beneficial insects and release them into your garden. As long as they can find their preferred prey in your garden, they will stick around. Such insects include ladybugs, lacewing flies, and praying mantises, all of which can be found at nurseries and garden supply stores.

Tobacco Spray

When I really needed to control a "bad bug," I collected wild tobacco leaves and cooked them in a pot of water. The concoction would typically be about two cups of leaves to about a gallon of water. Once it's cooled, I strain out the water, add a small amount (about a teaspoon) of liquid detergent, and put it into a spray bottle. I use this nicotine poison selectively to kill off bugs.

Other Sprays

I have also collected earwigs when I had an invasion of them, put them in a blender, and blended them with water. I usually add some garlic because it helps to further repel insects. I strain out the solids, put the liquid in a spray bottle, and spray it on the problem areas. I originally heard about this in one of the Rodale publications—probably in *Organic Gardening* magazine—and have tried it off and on for years. It seems to be somewhat effective, although I dislike having to collect all the bugs and crush them in the same blender in which I also make milkshakes!

Hot Water

You can sometimes just spray the bugs off your plants, and this will temporarily stop the insect infestation. I have done this with aphids that infest roses and citrus trees. Obviously, this is more practical with smaller gardens. When the hose has been lying out in the sun on a hot day, you will have just a few minutes worth of very hot water that you can use to spray off the aphids. You can also use a spray bottle filled with hot water.

Eggshells

Eggshells should never be tossed into the trash. Because they are primarily calcium carbonite, they can be ground up and added around any plants that might need calcium. If crushed coarsely and added around plants that are being eaten by snails, the eggshells will deter the snail attacks. It is difficult for them to slide over the sharp edges of the shells. (Yes, I said "difficult," not "impossible.")

GARDEN ACCESSORIES

In one of my gardening classes, a student revealed that she doesn't garden as much as she'd like to because "it costs too much." This came as a shock to me. Part of why I enjoy gardening—besides the fact that it produces food and a wonderful atmosphere around the home—is that I don't need to buy anything!

If you need pots or containers, there are countless things we routinely discard that can be used for potting plants or raised beds, such as old cans, pieces of wood, old trash cans, bathtubs, old dishpans, and so on. Trellises for tomatoes or peas can be made from any sticks and twine. (True, my yard does not look like the trophy yards in the slick gardening magazines.)

Ron Wilson of Eagle Rock, California, recently showed me what he did with old chain-link fences that were removed when he remodeled his yard. He mounted some on the wall of his house, one as a "ceiling" for a walkway, and then planted vines to grow over it. He found an ideal use for the old chain-link fence and didn't need to spend a hundred dollars for a comparable "trellis" at a garden supply store.

*An old milk carton
makes a suitable
temporary planter.*

*A retaining wall made
from stacked pieces of
old sidewalk.*

Ron Wilson's trellis over his side yard is made from an old section of chain-link fence.

CAREL STRUYCKEN'S METHODS

Carel Struycken has long been interested in the principles of permaculture, not only as it relates to growing fruits and vegetables, but also in his perspective of most human activities. Struycken has lived in Pasadena, California, for the past twenty-five years. He was born in Holland, grew up in Curacao in the Caribbean, and then moved back to Holland at age fifteen. We met in the summer of 2008 on the eve of his move to Catalina Island to discuss his efforts regarding home food production and permaculture.

He showed me Bill Mollison's *Permaculture: A Designers' Manual* (Tagari, 1997), which details a way to grow food and live with the land in accordance with nature's principles.

Carel Struycken with plums in his backyard permaculture garden.

"The whole idea of permaculture is to put in as little work as possible and allow nature to find its balance," says Struycken, who produced all the vegetables for a family of five for many years using these principles. "I'm also a big fan of Masanobu Fukuoka, author of *The One-Straw Revolution*. If I had the time, I'd love to go to Japan, work on his natural farm, and learn about his methods."

Both Mollison and Fukuoka are advocates of natural farming, which means planting what is appropriate for the area, tilling as little as possible, letting all the leaves and old plants serve as fertilizer for the new plants, and using natural methods for bug control. Using permaculture methods, Struycken grew many Asian greens, mostly those members of the mustard family that had the highest nutritional value. He also grew herbs, tomatoes, yard-long beans, and fourteen fruit trees.

His yard is terraced with cement rubble—pieces of old cement walkways that have been neatly stacked to form impressive and long-lasting walls. He also experimented with raised beds because the soil in his garden area was so bad. The smaller the plot, the harder it is to practice permaculture methods. Still, Struycken never raked up and discarded leaves.

The author with Carel Struycken.

Under his avocado tree, he allowed the leaves to accumulate into a thick layer of mulch. "The layer of avocado leaves is well over a foot thick, and when you look into the bottom of the pile, it is all naturally producing rich soil," he explains.

All the kitchen scraps were recycled in compost heaps, and he worked at cultivating the earthworms that naturally occurred in his yard so they would do the tilling. He purchased ladybugs years ago because they eat the "bad" insects, and he found that the ladybugs like the fennel plants. So the secret to keeping ladybugs around is to grow fennel, explains Struycken.

Permaculture does not involve raking away leaves or garden scraps but instead using them for the next generation of fertilizer. Although Struycken tried to produce all of his needed fertilizer from his own backyard, he occasionally needed to bring in chicken and horse manure for his crops. "I stopped using the horse manure, though," he says, "since I found that it produced too many weeds."

"I was always amazed that I never had to do anything to my lettuce, and it was always perfect. The ecosystem took care of itself," explains

Struycken grows a variety of food in his permaculture garden, including tomatoes.

Struycken. Alhough there were many spiders and bugs in the garden, whatever bugs ate his lettuce got eaten by some other bug. This is one of the basic principles of permaculture—nature, largely left alone, will find its own balance.

Struycken, who has been in the movie business for about thirty years, wants to do a series of documentaries where he shows sustainable communities throughout the world. By doing so, he hopes to preserve the principles of permaculture for new generations of gardeners. "The Amish are the most successful sustainable farmers, and they are using early eighteenth-century technologies," he says with a smile.

Struycken pauses to explain the difference between paleolithic and neolithic in order to make a point. "Humanoids have been around for at least a million years," he explains, "and modern humans have been here maybe five hundred thousand years. The paleolithics were the hunter/gatherers, and the neolithics were those who were settled in one place and who began agriculture. When we settled, we had to make the effort to force ourselves into the new mindset, but our true nature is paleolithic." He then shares a few comparisons to make his point.

The paleolithics lived in the here and now; they were more primitive by our standards, but they controlled their populations, had fewer taboos and laws, had fewer possessions, and managed to live on what the forest provided. He cites the Bushmen of the Kalahari as an example.

"When you had agricultural and cow-raising people who lived adjacent to the primitive people, the Bushmen would rarely die of hunger, though the agricultural people would die of hunger," says Struycken. "This is because the agricultural people learned to rely on and expect much more. When cattle died due to drought, for example, the agricultural people suffered far more than the Bushmen. The farmers also had to work a lot harder, usually seven days a week, whereas hunter/gatherers worked maybe three days a week."

Struycken cites the Bushmen and many others to illustrate that one of our "problems" is that we are so advanced that we have lost our primal paleolithic nature. Today, systems for gardening, farming, commerce, building, and more are all essentially neolithic and therefore unsustainable into the future. In this sense, Struycken believes that the details of our very survival can be gleaned by examining the details of sustainable societies. He is optimistic and believes that the solution to our problems is to properly understand the living principles of (so-called) primitive peoples.

LEARNING FROM THE FOREST

I was driving through a residential neighborhood of Los Angeles, just south of Griffith Park, when I saw a huge pile of wood chips dumped by a tree pruner on one of the front lawns. There was no actual front lawn per se—just swales of wood chips arranged in tiers on the gently sloping lot. A small chicken coop near the front held Rhode Island reds and banties. There were fruit trees, herbs, vegetables, and wild foods everywhere. Mushrooms sprouted from the wood chips. Various containers and composters were spread throughout the yard.

I walked up and was examining what seemed to be a recycled satellite dish turned into a solar cooker when David Kahn appeared. Kahn is an architect by trade whose thinking has led him down the path of natural architecture, using only natural materials. He is very concerned about diminishing resources in an ever-more populated world, and he is determined to be a living example and a part of the solution.

Kahn greeted me with a smile and handshake, and we began to talk and tour his "urban farm." He explained that more than half the world now lives in cities, and too many people have stopped learning how to live from nature. With more people using more resources, Kahn explained that we must rethink our approach to resources. This includes how we deal with trash, food production, waste production, and the rain that falls on our land, among other things. He was not trying to convince me of anything; rather, he was speaking like an evangelist literally engaged in the practice of saving the earth. He knew the specific details of what was happening in the "big picture," and he knew what each of us should do in our daily lives in order to be a part of the solution. Kahn is an optimist, not someone who is hollering about the impending end of the world as we know it. He explained his concern about the world at large and how he has chosen to be a part of the solution, right in his own urban yard.

"The choices that we make affect our world," said Kahn, "and most of our choices in terms of how we build houses, how we deal with trash, how we use energy, and how we raise our food, are all taking us down the wrong path. These are not sustainable paths, and we must begin to live the life that we believe is sustainable, good for the planet, and good for our health."

PERMACULTURE

In 2000, David Kahn discovered permaculture and eventually earned a permaculture certificate. "Permaculture" is a term coined by Bill Mollison (author of *Permaculture: A Designer's Manual*) derived from the phrase "permanent agriculture." Permaculture not only applies to sustainable patterns of agriculture, but also to building, transportation, economics, health, energy uses, and more. It is a way of studying nature and finding those patterns that are optimal not just for making money or producing food, but for the overall health and sustainability of humans, animals, and the land.

"Permaculture was the philosophy and action plan that tied all this together for me," says Kahn. He adds that permaculture is practiced all over the world, to differing degrees, and goes by many names. "Permaculture is essentially learning from nature and implementing that knowledge into everything we design. Permaculture is not new. It is ancient, using traditional methods to create sustainable communities in harmony with nature"

He then shows me that the leaves from his trees are not raked up but are instead left as a ground cover. They eventually decompose along with all the wood chips, compost, and chicken manure and become good soil. He holds a handful of the rich soil and tells me, "The most diverse design on the earth is the forest, and it's best if left alone." The forest recycles its own "waste" and thereby produces its own fertilizer for the growth of the trees. When the mulch is thick, water retention is high in the soil, so plants are better able to survive periods of drought. In fact, with rich soil, plants have also been shown to better survive periods of extreme cold. The key to the overall health of the system is good soil, and Kahn demonstrates that good soil can be produced by using everything found in the modern home and around the neighborhood.

"This is all about studying and emulating the patterns of nature," says Kahn, "and the relationships that plants and animals have with each other."

Soil

In my observation of how Kahn is able to produce so much food and fragrance, it is clear that he pays extra attention to the improvement of his soil. Large piles of wood chips are made into terraces on the slight slope of his property. As the wood chips decompose, mushrooms appear, showing that the underground mycelium is alive and breaking down the wood into usable soil. Bugs and worms are in evidence everywhere. The wood chips retain rainwater, and there is hardly any runoff from his property after a rain. He also lays sections of cardboard along the pathways; this "trash" not only quickly decomposes, but also produces edible mushrooms.

Compost

Kahn uses several compost systems to decompose both kitchen waste and yard trimmings. He has the conventional black plastic composters, as well as sections where the organic matter is placed in bulk to quickly convert it to soil. Kahn also teaches classes on his property, such as how to use chicken and horse manure to create a good fertilizer in seventeen days.

Chickens and Pigeons

One main chicken coop and one portable coop can be found on the Kahn homestead. His mix of chickens includes Rhode Island reds, banties, and others. He proudly shows me a few eggs from the day's collection: beautiful brown eggs and lovely bluish green–shelled eggs.

The chickens roam the yard each day, scratching around, eating bugs and worms, and depositing their fertilizer. Chickens can also be fed yard clippings and leftover kitchen scraps; they are therefore ideal to keep on a sustainable homestead.

He also has a coop where he raises pigeons, some of which he has eaten. Pigeons, also known as squab in some parts of the world, are quiet, produce a good fertilizer, and can be bartered or eaten.

Chickens in Kahn's yard.

Kahn feeds his chickens with freshly picked wild greens from his yard.

Eggs from Kahn's chickens.

Recycled Materials

"Nothing should be regarded as trash," says Kahn. "We are using up our resources, and it is necessary for us to refurbish and reuse things. We also need to find multiple uses for products and quit simply throwing things away."

Many of the planters around his yard are old metal, paper, or plastic containers that are now housing plants as these containers slowly decompose into his yard. His raised garden beds are made from old lumber. His solar cooker was created from an old satellite dish. The chicken coop is made from scrap lumber. There is an old brick incinerator on the property from the early days of Los Angeles when everyone burned their trash in

Food is cooked on a satellite dish that has been recycled into a solar cooker.

Edible weeds are allowed to grow as mulch and food. Kahn picks some fresh mallow greens for salad.

the backyard. Kahn will eventually replace it with a cobb oven, which will be designed to also heat water.

"Remember," says Kahn, "waste does not exist in nature. In a sustainable system, you need to go out of your way to find multiple uses for things. I will always go out of my way to use recycled materials, not only because it is right to do so, but also as an example to others."

Rain

Kahn calculated that 53,000 gallons of rain hit his 2,500-square-foot roof one season. All the water funnels to one downspout, and Kahn is in the process of upgrading his rain harvesting system. He has square plastic containers that can store 300 gallons each, five of which he plans to install on the south side of his house. The water will be used for agriculture, so he is not concerned about purifying it.

David Kahn's yard and lifestyle are not just some quirky ideas from the 1960s. He regards the principles of permaculture as one of the avenues of salvation for humankind, and he practices this on his own urban homestead. "We humans have exceeded the capacity of the planet," explains Kahn. "The most important thing we can do in our lifetime is to rectify the disparity on the planet that we have created. Nothing is more important. And it is criminal for the media and politicians to be in denial of this."

Kahn also says that because more and more of us live in cities, we must produce our food in the cities and we must live sustainable lives. "What I'm doing here is a snapshot of what the future will look like if we are to survive," says Kahn. "Nothing in my formal education prepared me for this. In school, we stopped learning about life and we focused on tiny ingredients without seeing how they all related. For me, permaculture tied everything together. It provided me with the blueprint to begin being and living the solution."

LIVING IN A TEPEE

Amy Woodruff has discovered that she can experience "being close to the land" in a tepee located in her Eagle Rock, California, backyard. Woodruff, who is of Choctaw and Cherokee descent, grew up on a family farm in Norco, California, where they raised their own food.

"We had a year-round garden and orchard where we raised oranges, peaches, and other fruit," she says. "We also raised and butchered our own chickens, rabbits, goat, sheep, and cows." But she explains that it was hard to kill animals that had names, and she more recently chose to adopt a vegan diet.

Before moving to Eagle Rock, Woodruff had been living in New York for four years doing photography and other jobs. Although she found New York exciting and fast-paced, she began to realize that there was also something missing. "I wanted to be close to the land," she says. "In New York, there wasn't even a front yard." When she moved to her current home, she was happy to have a place where she could grow a small garden and do her Native American craftwork.

*Woodruff's front-
yard tepee.*

Woodruff became interested in outdoor skills and primitive living arts and attended the Winter Count event in Arizona in February of 2007, a week-long gathering with daily classes in pottery, weaving, fire-making, wild plants, and other skills. "I began to realize how easy it was to live outdoors when I met people who lived in a traditional tepee," says Woodruff, who purchased her own tepee shortly thereafter.

The unique Native American tepee of the Great Plains has long been the focus of artists and even urban planners who recognize it as a uniquely economical shelter that is easy to cool and heat, and which provides an almost spiritual experience to those who live inside it. "I began to appreciate the tepee even more after I began to live in the tepee. It is really special to be able to see the stars at night through the smoke flap and hear

*At the entrance to
her tepee.*

birds in the morning," says Woodruff, as she glances around in her airy 16-foot-diameter tepee. She uses it for a bedroom and living room, and she also has a cooking grill in the middle where she can heat water or cook meals. She has only slept indoors for two months since she obtained the tepee over a year ago.

"I recently began to study kundalini yoga," she adds. "You really begin to find out who you are when you do yoga, and things from the past come up when you are working on yourself," she explains. Woodruff has been taking classes five times a week at the Golden Bridge Yoga Studio in nearby Hollywood.

"This has also inspired me to do research on my ancestry and on Native American culture in general," she explains, gesturing to the Native

Woodruff inside her tepee with a traditional drum she made.

American books in her bookcase. "In the big city of New York, it was different and there were things to explore, but it brought me back here. Being in New York made me realize that I already have it, it is all right here, now," she says, reverentially touching the grass floor of her tepee.

"I love it because I feel that I can be anywhere when I'm in here," she says. "I don't have to be in a front yard in Eagle Rock. I feel that this is sacred space, and I feel that it is so good to be out here on the mother earth. Even though I'm living in the city now, L.A. is good, and I'm only twenty minutes from the ocean and mountains, and only one hour away from the desert," she explains.

Woodruff creates Native American–inspired jewelry, such as leather belts, necklaces, purses, and clothing, which she sells at local shops and

Woodruff gardens in her yard and keeps a compost pit for recycling kitchen waste and raising earthworms.

online at www.daughterofthesun.net. She is currently building a "gypsy wagon"—an approximately 8 by 16 feet–house truck that will essentially be a workshop on wheels. It will allow her to travel to different art shows and other gatherings around the country where she displays and sells her work.

As for what Woodruff's neighbors think about her tepee, she says, "I had the tepee up since March of '07, but I didn't really get any reactions until Halloween of last year when the tepee was open for the trick-or-treaters. Everyone said they loved it and they wanted their children to look inside. Everyone was very supportive of it."

Picking earthworms out of a compost pit.

Feeding earthworms to her water turtles.

Woodruff offers simple advice to other city folks who also want to experience a little of her self-reliant lifestyle. "Begin by doing simple things like composting your kitchen scraps to make good soil. And grow some of your own food, even in pots. Dry your clothes in the sun on a clothesline, and use cotton napkins that you wash. The most important thing is to educate yourself so you learn what you can do in your own home and yard," says Woodruff.

9

GETTING
AROUND

When we're stuck on the freeway with cars going 5 mph, or not moving at all, we start to wonder about the wonders of our modern life. We spend tens of thousands of dollars to purchase a vehicle, hundreds more each year for upkeep and maintenance, and increasingly more dollars every week for fuel. No wonder so many of us have begun to wonder: What am I doing this for? Is this worth it?

I recall a humorous cartoon from an anti-car, pro-bicycle magazine. A man is stuck in bumper-to-bumper traffic on a freeway, telling his passenger, "I need my car to get to my job." In the next scene, he is sitting in his packed cubicle at work, prisonerlike, telling his cubicle buddy, "I need my job to pay for my car."

A sad but true commentary on the "life" we have created for ourselves.

Let's just think back a few thousand years. Ancient Greek philosophers write of travel, but how did they get around? For the most part, they walked! Sure, there were horses if one could afford the upkeep, and there were boats if a waterway defined the desired route. In general, however, people planned walking time into their shopping and visiting. Cities were a bit more compact, and they were designed around the ability to get from one place to another on foot or by horse. Most walking journeys were shorter than ten miles, which was considered normal.

When was the last time you walked ten miles? When was the last time you walked around your block and explored your neighborhood? It is truly amazing the adventures that await the neighborhood walker. We tend not to see what is right under our noses. In urban and suburban areas, we drive to the store even if it is only a mile away. Yet an average person can walk a flat mile in under twenty minutes!

I recently walked around my old neighborhood to advertise a local farmer's market that I was managing. In a little over two hours, I walked about six miles. Some of the parts of my neighborhood were wholly unknown to me. Some parts were scary indeed, and I'd never go there at night. Other parts were remarkably idyllic, as if I'd fallen into another parallel universe. My walk was a tangible connection to the people and land where I lived; I felt good when I was finished. It had been a very cold day, and everyone else seemed to be shivering in their wraps and thick coats, while I was comfortable in my light sweater. These are just some of the many benefits of walking.

BICYCLES

The only self-powered traveling device worth mentioning is the bicycle. Some pedal-cars exist, but none have risen to the same level of practicality and safety as the bicycle, except perhaps within the confines of a large estate or on flat farmland. The bicycle is perhaps the most efficient means of transportation available.

Bicycles are relatively inexpensive, reasonably easy to maintain in good working order, and require next to no outlay of cash on a regular basis. For short distances, there are many carts available for carrying children or pets. There are also numerous racks (and packs) that you can use for carrying whatever necessary items to a job site, school, or out shopping.

Many people do not bicycle because their homes and jobs are an hour or more apart, requiring a freeway drive. Unlike many European towns, most American cities are spread out with the assumption that people will drive anywhere they need to go. So much for the idea of "urban planning"; this lack of people-planning has made living ecologically more difficult, as most people cannot walk or bicycle to work.

Although American cities have grown and sprawled, we as individuals can make choices to find work closer to home and support local merchants. Additionally, it's possible in today's world to do much of our shopping and work at home through online shopping and telecommuting. If you are able to take advantage of such resources, you won't have to leave your home at all unless you choose to.

BENEFITS OF A BICYCLE

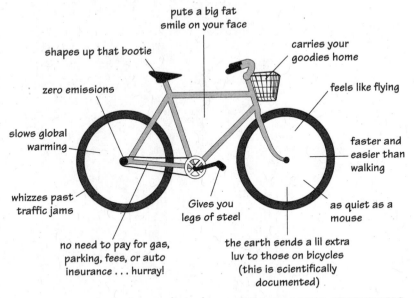

puts a big fat
smile on your face

shapes up that bootie

carries your
goodies home

zero emissions

feels like flying

slows global
warming

faster and
easier than
walking

whizzes past
traffic jams

Gives you
legs of steel

as quiet as a
mouse

no need to pay for gas,
parking, fees, or auto
insurance . . . hurray!

the earth sends a lil extra
luv to those on bicycles
(this is scientifically
documented)

REPRINTED WITH PERMISSION FROM C.I.C.L.E., WWW.CICLE.ORG

RAFAEL GOMEZ'S MISSION

Pasadena, California, resident Rafael Gomez rides his bicycle 365 days a year, rain or shine. He is a passionate advocate for bicycling—bicycling for health, bicycling for youth, bicycling to save the planet. Although a lifelong bicyclist, it was not until he returned from the Vietnam War that he and his brother Vicente became serious bicycle racers. "After returning to the states, we used bicycling as a form of self-therapy, as our positive way to overcome the stress of serving in an unpopular war," explains Gomez.

Of Yaqui Indian heritage, Gomez refers to his bicycle as his "steel pony." He says, "Too many of the youth today see their only transportation as a car. Our whole culture pushes youth that way, and that's too bad. And did you know that one of the best training sites for bicycle racers is right here in our own backyard? Right here in the Arroyo Seco on Pasadena's west side, home of the Rose Bowl, is the best place to practice bike racing west of the Mississippi."

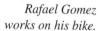

Rafael Gomez works on his bike.

His religion is the bicycle, his church the open road, and his holy of holies is the Arroyo Seco–Rose Bowl area. Promoting bicycling is Rafael Gomez's primary mission in life. "I'd like to see grammar school teachers bring their whole classes to watch bicycle races—both the boys and girls. Let the children see it and be inspired by it," exclaims Gomez. "The children need to see adults involved in bicycling. The adults need to set the example so children grow up wanting to be on a bike. With the advent of the electric car in this country, we started to lose the great importance of bicycling. Today, people in Third World countries have a much better perspective on bicycling than we do.

"Cycling truly helps the world. It's an environmentally safe form of transportation. There's no noise, it's safe, and it keeps you strong. Riding a bike is far better than a car or even the bus. Riding puts you in touch with nature in a way that riding an auto can never do," he says enthusiastically. When you look at the fire in his eye, you can sense that to this Yaqui in the modern world, his bike is truly his pony in the urban wilderness.

Rafael Gomez has found his fountain of youth via his bicycle. He becomes one with his machine as he communes with nature and the road. His lungs pump oxygen through his body, heart, and brain as he propels by one-people-power through the streets of southern California. He does not fear gas shortages or automobile breakdowns. He has learned that by transporting himself on this simple wheeled device, he accomplishes many things at once: he stays in top shape and peak health, he does not contribute to environmental pollution, and he needs no gym or psychologist. Rafael Gomez lives the life of health.

RICHARD REDMAN'S COMMUTE

Seventy-year-old Richard Redman of Altadena, California, is glad that riding his bicycle to work is good for the environment. He also rides his bicycle because he enjoys it and it makes him feel good. "Yes, it's wonderful to do something that's good for the environment. I like that," he says. "But I also feel good, and I sleep well, and I have lots of energy."

Since the summer of 2000, Redman has bicycled eleven miles to work and back, a total of about twenty-two miles a day. He bicycles five days a week, thirty-four weeks out of the year, when he is teaching at Franklin High School in Highland Park (a hilly district of Northeast Los Angeles). Outside of going to school and coming home, he also rides about twenty to thirty extra miles each week.

Environmental activist and actor Ed Begley, Jr. states that one of the single best things you can do to help the environment is to get out of your car at least one day a week and either walk, bicycle, carpool, or take the bus. Clearly, Richard Redman is doing his share and more.

I wondered, however, about the practicality of bicycling to one's job every day. It might not be easy or practical for everyone. In fact, Redman found that running was his passion. He ran regularly in the Arroyo Seco canyon, which is adjacent to his home. Hikers and strollers would see

*Richard Redman
with his bicycle.*

Redman on a regular basis running up and down the mountain trails, about forty miles a week. When training for a marathon, he would run seventy miles a week; he actually ran over three thousand miles one year. "But then my knees just gave out. It became very painful to run," he explains. "If my knees hadn't given out, I'd still be running every day, and I'm not sure I'd bicycle to school every day."

Prior to 2000, Redman had been teaching at Los Angeles High School, located about four miles west of downtown Los Angeles on Olympic Boulevard and about twenty miles from his home. "I was teaching at L.A. High for a total of eight years, and I found that each year it took another one to two minutes to get there driving. I could see the traffic gradually getting worse, and it really upset my psyche. A colleague told me about an opening for a biology teacher at Franklin High School, which was close enough to my home for me to bicycle. I applied for that position and got it."

In other words, Redman was open to working closer to home, and he remained open to possibilities that would enable him to live the life that would be more conducive to his health awareness. He began riding his Cannondale road bike to school and back, never using a bike rack, but carrying whatever gear he needed in his backpack. "I never cared much for a bike rack," he explains, "and if I ever needed to carry a heavy load to school, I simply drove my car." Fortunately, he has a locker at his school where he keeps a change of clothes for his teaching day.

His bicycle route is largely downhill to his school, so it takes about forty minutes to get there. The course he planned takes him through scenic areas in all but a mile-and-a-half stretch when he rides down busy York Boulevard. He takes the reverse route home every day, with a slight uphill grade, taking about sixty minutes to get home.

He wears a helmet and a bright yellow bicycling outfit for safety. An automobile once hit him and knocked him off his bike. Although the motorist who hit Redman quickly drove off, other motorists stopped and helped him, and he suffered only minor bruises. He has not experienced any serious problems with dogs, since he can outride them. During periods of heavy rain, he simply drives his car to work.

Redman is one of the few teachers at his school who rides his bicycle, and he estimates that there are—amazingly—only five to ten students who bicycle. (When I was in high school, there were well over a hundred of us who bicycled to school, in our school of about 3,000 students.) While the students nearly all live nearby, Redman believes that part of the reason more students don't bicycle is fear of vandalism or theft, even though the school has a special enclosure for bicycles.

"Sometimes [the students] ask me if I have a car, and I tell them 'yes,'" says Redman. "Then the student will ask me why I don't drive the car, and I tell them that I find it more enjoyable to ride a bike. They don't laugh at me, and I think some of them just think I'm stupid. In other words, in the mind of a high school student, why would you ride a bike when you could drive a car? Some students do say that I'm weird or crazy."

Redman's fellow teachers have slightly different opinions on his bicycling. "Some say they feel guilty for not bicycling. Some say they are envious. Others have told me that they feel that they should be bicycling, too," he says. "Sometimes, people have told me that they admire me for bicycling. So I ask them, 'So what is stopping you from doing it too?' and usually they don't say anything."

Redman emphasizes safety in bicycling, both in the color of his outfit and in the route that he has carefully selected to go to school each day. He also points out that bicycling isn't exactly free. "I probably spend $500 to $600 a year on repairs, bike clothing, and tires. "I would say that I probably spend $100 to $200 per year on just tires and tubes. Remember, I am riding 5,000 to 6,000 miles a year."

Redman is one of the new pioneers in living lightly on the earth, being a part of the solution to our global ills. He has proven that all one needs to do is make a commitment, and then find ways to live the life one wants.

Bicycle Choice

The best bike to purchase, as always, depends on your budget, your needs, and your tastes. You should also take into account how the bike feels when you ride it, as well as ease of repair. There are lots of new developments in bicycle manufacturing, so today's recommendation is tomorrow's old news. You can get some advice from Consumer Reports, or just ask around at bike shops and among your bike-riding friends.

SMALL GAS SCOOTERS

Jay Watkins of Pasadena discovered the viability of small gas-powered bikes some years ago and had acquired five of them at last count. He invited me to lunch one day, and when I arrived, he informed me that we'd be motor-biking there. I initially balked at the suggestion, but when I finally got on the bike, I found the experience to be pleasant and relatively safe, and the bike used just a fraction of the foreign oil that an automobile would have required.

My wife Dolores also drove a Vino gas-powered motor bike, which is manufactured by Yamaha and gets about 150 to 160 miles a gallon, according to Dolores's estimate. She needed to get a license for this motor bike but said she felt a bit safer on the Vino than on her smaller electric E-Go bike.

Dolores on her gas-powered Vino.

Safety is the biggest issue for most people when considering whether or not to drive a motorcycle. Motorcycles—especially small ones—give us far more mileage per gallon than our larger automobiles.

ELECTRIC SCOOTERS

The electric scooter is for those trips that are too far for walking or when you just don't think your body can handle the bicycle. The viability of the electric scooter has been highly underestimated. Think about it! You can plug your bike into a socket—which could be powered by your solar electric array—and then you travel around using no fuel whatsoever.

I must admit that I thought these were more of a novelty until I met several people who use them frequently and speak highly of the experience.

Scooters are not for long trips but instead are for trips around town, to the post office, the store, or anywhere in between. The biggest challenge, I think, is merging with regular traffic and making certain you stay safe. Electric scooters are easier and cheaper than a motorcycle to ride, and parking is always simple to the extreme.

Dolores drove an electric E-Go bike (manufactured by the Kin Sui Cheng Industrial Company), which she used for shopping within a few-mile radius from her home. If she used it a lot, she would plug it in each night, enabling it to run for 40 to 50 miles per charge. Electric scooters do not require the owners to have a license. "I really like riding it," stated Dolores when I asked her about it. "I'm a little worried about traffic, so I stay on the side streets."

Dolores set a good example for those who are still stuck inside their cars. She rode her E-Go or her Vino regularly to the store, until her recent death at age 62, proving that such alternate vehicles are not just for teenagers.

ELECTRIC CARS

Electric cars have been around for a long time, but many still do not go fast enough to take them on the freeway. As fuel prices rise, more electric cars will make their way into mainstream transportation. Today, they are most viable if you don't have to travel on the freeway and if your commute is under fifty miles round-trip.

Probably the greatest current hurdle for the mass introduction of electric cars is the high initial cost and the relatively low speed on highways. Some of the more practical electric cars I have seen are also very small vehicles, similar to early Volkswagen bugs or glorified golf carts—cheap to operate but potentially dangerous on the road.

Are electric cars feasible for the masses? Maybe. Sometimes we, as individuals and society as a whole, do not apply our minds to finding better ways of doing things until the more conventional methods become too costly and impractical. As gas prices rise and we become increasingly aware of the political ramifications of getting our fuel, electric cars powered by the sun seem like a no-brainer. If and when the industry's technicians realize this, we'll see new technologies improve so that more of us can move about in practical electric cars.

The Zapcar, one of the electric cars now available. See them at www.zapworld.com.

BIODIESEL

If you have a diesel engine vehicle, you might consider making your own fuel. According to some estimates, about 250,000 cars on the roads of America today are powered by vegetable oil fuel.

I spoke with Gabriel Hines of La Crescenta, California, who has been making his own fuel for years. Gabriel Hines is one of the New Pioneers in the quiet revolution. He taught himself how to make fuel for his diesel vehicle, and he has driven his vehicle at least 10,000 miles from oil that he processed, which would have otherwise been discarded from a local family-run restaurant.

Hines initially got interested in making his own fuel because he wanted to maximize his fuel efficiency, and he had heard lots of people talking about how economical it was to do this. He already had a diesel-powered Volkswagen pickup Rabbit, which got about 50 miles per gallon. He also liked the idea that he could safely store his homemade fuel in his yard, which he could not do with diesel (the flash point of diesel is 185 degrees F, whereas the flash point of vegetable fuel is 395 degrees F). When he decided to try making his own fuel, Hines went online and spent about ten hours studying the details of this process. Most of his research was done at www.journeytoforever.org, a site operated by Mike Pelliel. He then went to a local restaurant, told them what he was intending to do, and they gave him 5 gallons of their used vegetable oil.

"The first time I tried this was the hardest because I was still learning about it," says Hines. "But I did it right the first time and used the fuel in my car." The second batch he made, however, was too gelatinous and globby, and he didn't put it into his car. He researched what he might have done wrong and discovered that he added too much lye in the process. He corrected his procedure, and then standardized the way he makes the fuel so that all proportions are figured based on beginning with five gallons of

Gabriel Hines prepares to process used vegetable oil into auto fuel for his diesel vehicle.

used vegetable cooking oil. Since then, he has not had any problems with his procedure and has made about two hundred loads of diesel fuel.

There are several ways to make and use vegetable oil in a diesel car.

1. Pour pure oil directly into the diesel vehicle, without processing the oil or changing the engine. This is not the common method for several reasons. Although you could just pour pure peanut oil into the tank of a diesel vehicle, it is not economical. At the time of this writing, new peanut oil is at least twice as costly as diesel fuel. Also, although the pure oil would likely not damage the vehicle, it may be hard to start—it will take longer for the glow plugs to heat the fuel, and it may take five times as long to get the car started.

2. You can mix diesel fuel from the gas station with strained vegetable oil in an approximately 50/50 ratio, with no modification required on the engine. This means you are cutting your fuel cost in half, but you could always go back to pure diesel if you had to.

3. Add a separate tank that uses diesel, and use the main tank for pure, strained vegetable oil (typically, old used oil). This method requires some work on the vehicle and fuel lines so it all works well together. You start the car with diesel until the engine is warmed up, then you switch over to the vegetable fuel oil and run the car on it. Before you shut off the engine, you switch back to the diesel so the fuel lines have diesel in them to make the next start easier. This method is more common, and there are books and workshops on how to do this. Several of the people I spoke to liked *Biodiesel Homebrew Guide* by Maria "Girl Mark" Alovert. There are also mechanics who specialize in making this adjustment to a diesel vehicle.

4. You can buy processed vegetable oil, called biodiesel, either pure or mixed in varying degrees with diesel. Some gas stations are even beginning to sell biodiesel. Many people are interested in the idea of supporting the production of a homegrown fuel, but they do not have the time or the inclination to do it themselves.

5. You can process the used vegetable oil yourself. This is the option that Gabriel Hines has chosen, and the option that we'll describe. This method is referred to as transestifying the oil. You are taking the sugars and starches out of the used vegetable oil so it will not harm or clog any parts of the diesel engine.

Hines has used this method for over a year, driving more than 10,000 miles using his homemade biodiesel that he makes in five-gallon batches. He has made no modifications to the car, nor has he ever changed the timing. One online site that advises people on using biodiesel recommends a slight change in timing. Hines found that his car ran fine as it was, however, and he never had to make any adjustments.

To make his biodiesel, Hines first goes to a local restaurant and gets at least five gallons of used vegetable oil. He has never had to pay for this oil. He notes that the oil from "Mom and Pop" restaurants is of better quality than the oil discarded from fast-food chains. This is because fast-food chains use their oil much longer, which might make you reconsider eating at such a place.

Hines checks the temperature; it needs to be 140 degrees F.

The unstrained oil is then poured into an aluminum cooking pot and heated on a commercial turkey fryer. Turkey fryers can usually be purchased at any large building supply store. It is powered by a propane tank, which costs about 20 dollars to refill.

Hines heats the oil to 140 degrees F. The ideal temperature is actually between 120 and 130 degrees, but in the process of doing each step, Hines notes that the oil will cool slightly and end up being within the ideal temperature range when he is ready to proceed.

He checks the pH of the oil using a digital pH-checker called Aqua-Check, available at pool supply stores. The pH level determines how much lye he adds in the next step. The pH level needs to be between 8 and 9 for a finished biodiesel batch (8.3 is ideal). When I observed Hines making a batch, his waste oil from the restaurant had a pH that measured 6.8.

Hines checks the pH of the oil. The pH level determines how much lye should be added to the oil.

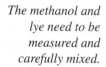

The methanol and lye need to be measured and carefully mixed.

The next step is to mix lye with methanol in a separate, clean bucket. The amount of lye to be added is determined by the oil's pH. The amount of methanol is 20 percent of your intended volume. Hines therefore pours one gallon of methanol into a separate bucket. (One gallon is 20 percent of the five-gallon expected total.)

Hines wears plastic gloves and a face mask because lye is very caustic, and any splashing will cause a burn. To determine how much lye to measure, he consults a chart he devised. The chart takes into account that he uses five gallons for his standard batch. "I rounded up my chart, and it's really quite simple," he says. "I fluctuate between about 6 grams every decimal. It's not a perfect chart, but for a five-gallon batch (yielding four usable gallons), this chart could be followed with no problems. This should give people a good idea of how much lye is needed per five-gallon batch."

*Pouring methanol
into a clean
bucket.*

Based on his oil's pH of 6.8 and his five-gallon standard, he needed to add 113.5 grams of lye in order to adjust the pH to the desired 8.3. The 113.5 grams of lye is carefully measured out into a small container and weighed on a digital postal scale.

The 113.5 grams of lye is then carefully poured into the bucket holding the gallon of methanol. Using a paint mixer attached to the end of drill, Hines then blends the lye crystals into the methanol for about five minutes or until all the crystals are dissolved. He has processed his own fuel so often that he notices a slight change in color when the mix is ready (from clear to slightly brown), as well as a unique odor resulting from the reaction between the lye and methanol.

Measuring out the lye.

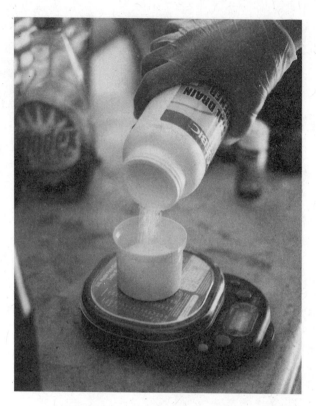

AMOUNT OF LYE NEEDED TO BRING pH TO A DESIRABLE LEVEL

Mixture's Current pH	Lye Needed (in grams)
6.5	125
6.6	119
6.7	113
6.8	106
6.9	100
7.0	94
7.1	88

The methanol and lye are mixed.

Hines uses a paint mixer to combine the lye and methanol.

He then checks the temperature of the heated vegetable oil and slowly and carefully pours it into the plastic bucket with the methanol-lye mix. The oil is poured into the bucket until the mixture reaches his five-gallon mark on the inside of the bucket. Using the paint mixer on his drill, he begins to mix the entire contents of the bucket. He works the bottom of the bucket for about five minutes, then he puts a lid with a hole in the middle on the bucket so the paint mixer can be used while the bucket is covered. This final mixing takes at least thirty minutes, but sometimes Hines mixes it for about forty-five minutes.

Ready to pour the heated vegetable oil into the lye-methanol mix

"In the beginning, I would stand there for forty-five minutes with the drill in my hand," he says. Later, he set up a rig using another bucket so that he could just tape down the trigger of the drill and let it go on its own for thirty to forty-five minutes. Once the mixing is completed, the bucket is simply set aside for at least eight hours.

Hines showed me a bucket of this mixture that had already sat for eight hours. There was a very small amount of residue on the top that was easily skimmed off. Hines then carefully poured the finished biodiesel into a separate clean bucket. Out of the original five gallons, slightly over four

Carefully pouring the heated oil into the bucket with the lye-methanol mix.

Hines blends the contents with a drill for about forty-five minutes. When finished, he covers the bucket and sets it aside for at least eight hours.

After eight hours, a little bit of residue remains at the top of bucket. The residue is easily skimmed off.

Inspecting the nearly finished biofuel.

Hines carefully pours the contents into a clean bucket, being careful not to mix up the waxy material that has settled to the bottom in a mass.

The final pour.

gallons of usable fuel was produced. As he slowly poured the biodiesel, he was careful not to pour out any of the residue that had settled into a gel at the bottom of the first bucket, which was mostly a semisolid mass with a soapy texture. That residue is either discarded or used in other craft projects such as soap-making or fire-making devices for camping trips. Hines usually returns the bottom residue to the restaurant that it came from and they discard it.

Then, with a big smile, Hines held up his final product, ready to be poured into the tank of any diesel vehicle.

A happy Hines shows off about four gallons of homemade fuel for his diesel vehicle.

The Volkswagen diesel Rabbit that Hines fueled on recycled vegetable fuel for about a year.

DIANE DEREK'S MODIFIED CAR

Diane Derek, a school teacher in Alhambra, drove a standard diesel 1988 model 190D Mercedes. She says, "As gas and diesel prices began to rise quite dramatically this past year, I could see that this was just the beginning. It was clear that transportation by auto would continue to be quite expensive, and choosing to run my car on recycled vegetable oil was my way of saying 'no' to rising prices."

Although she didn't know anyone else who had converted their diesel cars to run on vegetable oil, she began to make personal inquiries and do online research. She found that people were eager to share their knowledge and experience. She eventually met several people in the local area

Diane Derek next to her diesel Mercedes, modified to run on waste vegetable oil.

who had been using waste vegetable oil (WVO) for their fuel in the Los Angeles area.

"Whenever there is some aspect of using WVO that I am unclear about, these people provide a wealth of experienced knowledge," says Derek. "It is almost impossible to *not* find information on the Internet on just about any subject. So, before I had my car modified, I read many chatroom forums that were created for people who use WVO in their diesels. I found this to be a helpful source of information, as many people described their trial-and-error experiences and offered simple solutions to those who encountered a problem. I found all the necessary 'how-to' aspects online."

After all her in-depth research, Derek purchased a dual-tank system from Greasecar. Then, using the online site Craigslist, she hired a mechanic who was knowledgeable about the system to install it. The conversion kit cost $1,200 and the installation cost her about $500.

The Greasecar Vegetable Oil Conversion System is an auxiliary fuel modification system that allows one to run a diesel engine on straight vegetable oil in any climate. The system includes a smaller tank (nine to ten gallons) installed in the wheel well for the vegetable oil, and the larger, original tank (about thirteen gallons), which continues to be used for diesel fuel.

Derek's car is started on diesel (when the engine is cold). After several miles, the aluminum-heated fuel cell is ready for the WVO, and Derek must push a switch mounted on the dashboard to change to the vegetable fuel. The engine is then running on pure WVO. Before turning off the engine, the same switch is used to "purge" the WVO from the lines so the engine will be ready to resume again on straight diesel fuel.

Other than this ritual of starting on diesel, switching to WVO after a few miles, and then switching back to diesel just before each stop, Derek operates her car as she did before. Except she rarely goes to the gas station to get her fuel. Derek gets her used oil from Asian restaurants that would otherwise discard it. "Most Asian restaurants use 100-percent vegetable oil to cook their food," explains Derek. "When the restaurant changes its cooking oil, it is usually poured in a fifty-five-gallon drum in the back of the restaurant. I tell the manager or owner what I use WVO for, and I ask if it is okay to take some of their waste oil. Nearly all of the responses are positive. My source is mostly from small restaurants that use soybean oil. After

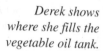

Derek shows where she fills the vegetable oil tank.

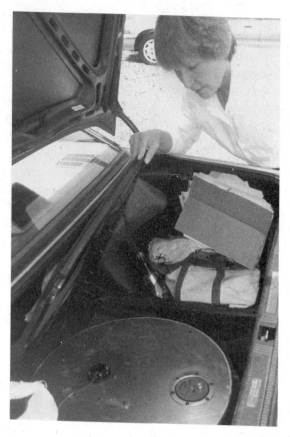

pumping the WVO from the large fifty-five-gallon drum into plastic 'cubies' (new vegetable oil is sold in 4.6-gallon cubies), I let it settle for several weeks in the sun. If there is any water residue, it will separate and collect in the bottom along with any bits of debris from cooking. The oil is strained to about one micron. I use paper towels and cotton cloth placed over a colander. There are large premade 'sock' filters that can be purchased to hang over large drums that filter the oil. However, with my limited space, this makeshift system is rather tidy and works for me."

Using this method, Derek filters about seven gallons a week without much effort. Now that she runs her car on vegetable oil, she notes that she hasn't had any problems with the performance of the car. In the event that she wants to take a cross-country trip where she is not certain of a steady supply of used vegetable oil, she can switch back to diesel. According to Derek, "The WVO tank can be removed and the car is back to factory condition because there is no modification made to the diesel fuel system."

"Anyone who wants to pursue this form of alternate fuel needs to keep in mind that there is a learning curve," says Derek. "For example, the oil must not contain water and must be nonhydrogenated, as that can cause problems. And it takes a little experience to know what the oil should look like before you go to the trouble of collecting it. Also, it can be a little time-consuming to collect and filter the oil. But like me, you might see that this is all worthwhile considering the price of diesel fuel. There are also single-tank conversion systems that cost about $700. If you're like me and drive about 7,000 miles a year, that system would pay for itself in about six months. Mine took a little longer to pay for itself, but I feel secure having both fuel systems operating independently of each other.

"I never tire from the aroma of fried food wafting in through the windows as I drive my vegetable fuel–powered car down the road," she adds. "In fact, driving my car with the windows down is reminiscent of being inside a restaurant. It can create an appetite."

GOOD FOR THE SOUL

The pursuit of self-reliance is good for the soul. We learn things of intrinsic value by relying on natural resources to sustain our lifestyles. We learn about ourselves, our environment, each other, and the unique complexity of our economy. We also learn that self-reliance is a state of mind and being. It is not something that money can buy. It is something that we earn, experience, and thereby enrich not just ourselves but our entire culture. Practicing self-reliance—a little or a lot—is good for the soul, and it's also good for society. When the individuals of any society choose to be wise stewards of their resources and get more out of less, the integrity of the ecology and economy are strengthened. "Living lightly on the land" is intrinsically good. Whether or not such a lifestyle will avert global warming, changes in weather, or other ecologic catastrophes is unknown. I do it because I feel it is right.

Over thirty years ago, I became interested in sustainable lifestyles when I began to garden, compost, recycle, and learn about wild foods.

I was attracted to WTI Inc., a nonprofit educational organization in the Los Angeles area. The founder has continued to be a source of education and inspiration, and the unique people I met at that time in my life have inspired me to this day.

This book is not meant to cover what has already been covered in recent books, such as all the gardening and permaculture methods in *Extreme Simplicity: Homesteading in the City*, which I coauthored with Dolores Nyerges, or all the survival tips mentioned in *How to Survive Anywhere*.

Writing this book required me to meet people, go to their homes, and learn about the paths of self-reliance they have pursued. It has shown me that all our answers are out there if we only choose to pursue them intelligently and forthrightly.

I didn't know how this book would turn out when I began, because each person I met introduced me to someone else, who introduced me to someone else. So for me, this has been an eye-opening adventure to meet the people who are pursuing self-reliance, and to attempt to distill it down to its simplest components.

I could not have written this book without the help of the new pioneers of the quiet revolution. They are all brave and industrious people who are pioneers in their own right. It is to these pioneers that I devote this book.

Selected Resources

There are many references available on self-sufficient living, and I have used far more than what is listed. The resources listed are the cream of the crop and the ones that are most relevant to the topics discussed in this book.

BOOKS

Alovert, Maria. *Biodiesel Homebrew Guide.* Order at *www.localb100.com/book.html.*

Angier, Bradford. *Feasting Free on Wild Edibles.* Mechanicsburg, PA: Stackpole Books, 2002.

Auerbach, Leslie. *A Homesite Power Unit: Methane Generator.* Alternative Energy Systems, 1979.

Begley, Ed, Jr. *Living Like Ed: A Guide to the Eco-Friendly Life.* New York: Clarkson Potter, 2008.

Bradley, Fern, and Barbara Ellis, editors. *Rodale's All-New Encyclopedia of Organic Gardening: The Indispensable Resource for Every Gardener.* Emmaus, PA: Rodale Books, 1993.

Coyne, Kelly, and Erik Knutzen. *The Urban Homestead: Your Guide to Self-Sufficient Living in the Heart of the City.* Los Angeles, CA: Process, 2008.

Davidson, Joel. *The Solar Electric Home: A Photovoltaics How-to Handbook.* Ann Arbor, MI: Aatec, 1983.

Fry, L. John. *Practical Building of Methane Power Plants for Rural Energy Independence.* Santa Barbara, CA: Fry, 1974.

Fukuoka, Masanobu. *The One-Straw Revolution.* New York: NYRB Classics, 2009.

———. *The Road Back to Nature: Regaining the Paradise Lost.* Japan: Japan Publications, 1988.

Hackleman, Michael. *At Home with Alternative Energy.* Culver City, CA: Peace Press, 1980.

———. *Wind and Windspinners: A Nuts and Bolts Approach to Wind-Electric Systems.* Culver City, CA: Peace Press, 1977.

Harrison, Kathy. *Just in Case: How to Be Self-Sufficient when the Unexpected Happens.* North Adams, MA: Storey Publishing, 2008.

House, David. *The Biogas Handbook.* Aurora, OR: House Press, 2006.

Jaeger, Ellsworth. *Wildwood Wisdom.* Bolinas, CA: Shelter Publications, 1992.

Jenkins, David, and Frank Pearson. *Feasibility of Rainwater Collection Systems in California.* Riverside, CA: University of California Center for Water Resources, 1978.

Jenkins, Joseph. *The Humanure Handbook: A Guide to Composting Human Manure, Third Edition.* Grove City, PA: Jenkins Publishing, 1999.

Lancaster, Brad. *Rainwater Harvesting for Drylands.* Tucson, AZ: Rainsource Press, 2006.

Laubin, Reginald, Gladys Laubin, and Stanley Vestal. *The Indian Tipi: Its History, Construction, and Use.* Norman, OK: University of Oklahoma Press, 1989.

Matson, Tim. *The Book of Non-Electric Lighting.* Woodstock, VT: Countryman Press, 2008.

Mollison, Bill. *Permaculture: A Designers' Manual.* Tasmania, Australia: Tagari Publications, 1997.

Nelson, Melissa. *Original Instructions: Indigenous Teachings for a Sustainable Future.* Rochester, VT: Bear & Company, 2008.

Nyerges, Christopher, and Dolores Lynn Nyerges. *Extreme Simplicity: Homesteading in the City.* White River Junction, VT: Chelsea Green, 2002.

Nyerges, Christopher. *Guide to Wild Foods and Useful Plants.* Chicago, IL: Chicago Review Press, 1999.

Ramsey, Dan. *The Complete Idiot's Guide to Solar Power for Your Home.* Exton, PA: Alpha Publishing, 2007.

Rodale, J.I. *Complete Book of Composting.* Emmaus, PA: Rodale Press, 2000.

Schaeffer, John. *Real Goods Solar Living Source Book.* Boulder, CO: Gaiam Real Goods, 2007.

Shelter. San Francisco, CA: Ten Speed Press, 1990.

Sloane, Eric. *Eric Sloane's Weather Book.* Mineola, NY: Dover Publications, 2005.

Solar Energy International. *Photovoltaics: Design and Installation Manual.* British Columbia, Canada: New Society Publishers, 2004.

Thayer, Samuel. *The Forager's Harvest: A Guide to Identifying, Harvesting, and Preparing Edible Wild Plants.* Cleveland, NY: The Forager Press, 2006.

Tickell, Joshua. *From the Fryer to the Fuel Tank: The Complete Guide to Using Vegetable Oil as an Alternative Fuel.* Tickell Energy Consultants, 2000.

MAGAZINES

Home Power

Mother Earth News

Organic Gardening

Sunset

ONLINE RESOURCES

American Solar Energy Society
www.ases.org

CMS Magnetics
www.magnet4sale.com

International Association of Plumbing and Mechanical Officials
www.iapmo.org

Journey to Forever
www.journeytoforever.org

Solar Rating and Certification Corporation
www.solar-rating.org

Wind Data Logger
www.winddatalogger.com

Windstream Power
www.windstreampower.com

WTI
www.wtinc.info

ORGANIZATIONS

The Center for Urban Agriculture at Fairview Gardens
598 N. Fairview Avenue
Goleta, CA 93117
www.fairviewgardens.org

Eco-Home Network
4344 Russel Avenue
Los Angeles, CA 90027
http://ecohome.org

School of Self-Reliance
Box 41834
Eagle Rock, CA 90041
www.ChristopherNyerges.com

TreePeople
12601 Mulholland Drive
Beverly Hills, CA 90210
www.treepeople.org

Index

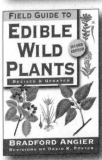